Improve your Skil

Reading *for IELTS*

with Answer Key

6.0–7.5

Jane Short

Macmillan Education
4 Crinan Street
London N1 9XW
A division of Macmillan Publishers Limited

Companies and representatives throughout the world

ISBN 978-0-230-46335-6 (with key)
ISBN 978-0-230-46344-8 (without key)
ISBN 978-0-230-46339-4 (with key + MPO Pack)
ISBN 978-0-230-46337-0 (without key + MPO Pack)

Text, design and illustration © Macmillan Publishers Limited 2014
Written by Jane Short

First published 2014

Designed by Kamae Design, Oxford
Illustrated by Kamae Design, p14, 23, 24, 29, 54, 56, 72, 76
Cover design by Macmillan
Cover image by Getty Images/AVTG
Picture research by Susannah Jayes

Author's acknowledgements
My partner, Bill, for his untiring support.

The publishers would like to thank all those who participated
in the development of the project, with special thanks to the
freelance editor.

The author and publishers would like to thank the following for
permission to reproduce their photographs:
Corbis p78(B), Corbis/Keith Levit/*/Design Pics p46(C); **Getty
Images** pp38(tl,cl,bl),70(A), Getty Images/FilmMagic p6(cm),
Getty Images/WireImage p6(cl); **ImageSource** pp46(A),70(C);
MACMILLAN AUSTRALIA p46(B); Photodisc p30(A),
Photodisc/Getty Images pp14(B),30(B),70(B); **Rex Features**/
Photofusion p78(A).

The author and publishers are grateful for permission to reprint
the following copyright material:
Material from: 'Social Media Privacy: A Contradiction in Terms?'
by Naomi Troni. Originally published on 24.4.2012 on Forbes.com.
Reprinted by permission of the publishers. www.Forbes.com.
Extract from: 'The Millenials: A New Generation of Employees,
A New Set of Engagement Policies' by Jay Gilbert. Originally
published in the Ivey Business Journal September 2011. Reprinted
by permission of the publishers. http://iveybusinessjournal.com
Material from 'Rapid Assessment of Drinking Water originally
published jointly by the World Health Organization and UNICEF
in October 2012. © *World Health Organization 2012.* Reprinted
by permission of the publishers. http://www.who.int/water_
sanitation_health/publications/2012/rapid_assessment/en/
Extract from 'Progress on drinking water and sanitation' originally
published jointly by the World Health Organization and UNICEF
in March 2012. © *UNICEF and World Health Organization 2012.*
Reprinted by permission of the publishers. http://www.who.int/
water_sanitation_health/publications/2012/jmp_report/en/

Extract from 'Beyond the Atmosphere: Early Years of Space
Science' by Homer Edward Newell published by NASA. Reprinted
by permission.
Extract from: 'People Who Are Alive Today Will Walk on Mars'
by Martin Rees. Originally published on the Times website on
9.8.2012. Reprinted by permission of the publishers
Material from: '**Creative strategies of Super Bowl
commercials 2001-2009: an analysis of message strategies**'
by Kihan Kim and Yunjae Cheong in The International Journal of
Sports Marketing & Sponsorship Vol 13 Issue 1, 2011 published by
IMR Publications. Reprinted by permission of the Publisher
Material from: '**Language Policy and Practice in Multilingual,
Transnational Families and Beyond**' by Li Wei in The Journal
of Multilingual & Multicultural Developement Vol 33 Issue 1, 2012
published by Taylor & Francis Journals. Reprinted by permission
of the Publisher
With kind permission from Springer Science + Business Media:
Extract from page 78-90 'Parental Roles' by Robert A.Veneziano
in 'The Encyclopaedia of Sex and Gender – Men and Women in
the World's Cultures'. Published by Kluwer Academic/Plenum
Publishers. © 2003 Kluwer Academic/Plenum Publishers, New York.
Material from 'Could Facebook help predict obesity hotspots?
Areas where people 'like' TV more than sport are less healthy' by
Emma Innes, originally published in The Mail Online 25.04.2013,
DailyMail.co.uk. Reprinted by permission of the Publisher.
Extract from: 'Their Social Life Online: A Parent's Guide' by Rachel
Carlyle. Originally published on the Times website on 17.11.2012.
Reprinted by permission of the publishers
Material from: 'Feeling in Control: Comparing Older People's
Experiences in Different Care Situations' by Lisa Callaghan and
Ann-Marie Towers in 'Ageing and Society', Firstview Article
published May 2013. Published by Cambridge University Press.
Reprinted by permission of the Publisher.
Material from 'Older Workers in the Labour Market, 2012'
published by the Office for National Statistics. Contains public
sector information licensed under the Open Government Licence
v2.0 (http://www.nationalarchives.gov.uk/doc/open-government-
licence/version/2/). © Crown Copyright 2012.
Extract from 'Work Longer, Live Healthier: The Relationship
between Economic Activity, Health and Government Policy' by
Gabriel Sahlgren. First published by the Institute of Economic
Affairs, London 2013.
Climate Change 2007: Impacts, Adaptation and Vulnerability.
Working Group II Contribution to the Fourth Assessment Report
of the Intergovernmental Panel on Climate Change, Ch. 16.5.5; Ch.
15.6.3. Cambridge University Press.
Routledge (T&F Journals)
Extract from 'The Link Between Child Nutrition and Health' by
Lesley Wood and Clare Harper, published by The Children's Food
Trust, August 2008. Reprinted by permission of the Publisher.
www.childrensfoodtrust.org.uk.
Extract from 'Food for Thought: Tackling Child Malnutrition to
Unlock Potential and Boost Prosperity' published by Save The
Children. © The Save the Children Fund 2013. Reprinted by
permission. www.savethechildren.org.uk

Printed and bound in the UK, by CLOC Ltd

2021 2020 2019 2018 2017
10 9 8 7 6 5 4 3

Contents

Introduction

What is *Improve your Skills: Reading for IELTS 6.0–7.5?*

Reading for IELTS is part of the *Improve your Skills* exam skills series: three preparation books which cover all aspects of the IELTS exam for students aiming for an IELTS band score of 6.0–7.5. This course aims to develop the key reading skills, and language and exam techniques for the IELTS Reading paper.

The course can be used together with the other books in the series: *Writing for IELTS 6.0–7.5* and *Listening & Speaking for IELTS 6.0–7.5*.

How do I use *Improve your Skills*?

You can use any of the books in this series either in class or to study on your own. The course will guide you through the activities step by step, so you can use this book with or without a teacher. If you are studying as part of a class, your teacher will direct you on how to use each activity. Some activities can be treated as discussions, in which case they can be a useful opportunity to share ideas and techniques with other learners.

How is *Improve your Skills: Reading for IELTS* organized?

The course is made up of 10 units, each aimed at developing a particular reading skill (e.g., *scanning*). Every unit is themed around a commonly occurring topic from the *IELTS* exam. Each unit consists of:

- **Skills development:** explanation, examples and tasks to develop and practise relevant reading skills both for general use and the exam. Each skill is broken down into simple stages with reference to why each skill is important for IELTS.
- **Vocabulary:** useful vocabulary for the IELTS exam.
- **Exam focus and practice:** focus on how each skill relates to the exam, followed by authentic IELTS-style tasks for real exam practice.

There are also *Skills tip* boxes throughout the book containing useful information and ideas on how to approach the different exam reading tasks.

How will *Improve your Skills* increase my chances of exam success?

Skills development

The skills sections form a detailed syllabus of core reading skills which are useful both in the exam and in everyday life – reading for specific information and understanding attitude and opinion, for example. People often do these things in their own language without noticing, so it can take some practice to perform these actions in another language. Learning and understanding vocabulary and grammar can take priority in the classroom, and these very important skills can often get ignored.

Language input

Each unit includes useful vocabulary and phrases for the exam. In *Improve your Skills: Reading for IELTS*, you will find a wide range of topic vocabulary and ideas to ensure that you are well prepared when you reach the real exam.

Exam technique

In any exam, it is important to be prepared for the types of tasks you are likely to be given, and to have methods ready to answer any particular question. The *Skills tip* boxes give short, simple advice about different types of questions, as well as study skills and how to effectively use the skills you have learnt. The course covers every question type that you will face in the IELTS exam.

How is the IELTS exam organized and where does reading fit in?

The IELTS exam consists of four papers: *Reading*, *Writing*, *Speaking* and *Listening*. The *Reading* paper consists of three reading passages with tasks (a total of 40 questions) and lasts one hour.

What does each task consist of?

The authentic reading passages are taken from a range of sources and aim to test your reading ability in a number of ways. The range of questions used in the exam are:

- multiple-choice questions
- short-answer questions
- sentence completion
- notes, flow chart, table completion
- labelling a diagram/map
- summary completion with and without wordlists
- classification
- matching information to paragraphs
- matching paragraph/section headings
- identification of information – True/False/Not Given
- identification of writer's views/claims – Yes/No/Not Given

You need to be comfortable with all of the question types, though there will probably only be a selection of them in the exam.

This course will develop your understanding of and strategies for answering all of the above question types, as well as the techniques you will need to use when reading, such as scanning and skimming.

How is it assessed?

The Academic Reading component is weighted, which means the number of correct answers required to achieve a particular band score may vary from exam to exam. As a rough guide, to achieve a score band 7, you should aim for at least 29 or 30 correct answers.

As you do different reading passages in the book, the number of correct answers in each will probably be different. This reflects the nature of the IELTS exam as some passages may appear to be easier or more difficult than others.

UNIT AIMS

READING SKILLS
Predicting content from textual clues
Finding key vocabulary
Skimming for topic
Identifying main ideas

EXAM PRACTICE
True/False/Not Given
Matching headings
Matching sentence endings

Will Smith

Lady Gaga

Predicting content

1 Look at these photos and answer the questions.
  a Why are these people famous?
  b What else can people do to become celebrities?
  c How many different types of media can you name?

Skills

Skimming

2 Quickly read the text below and underline the words associated with *celebrity* and the *media*.

> In the past, a person had to do something exceptional to be known as a famous figure: climb a mountain, row single-handedly around the world or fight bravely in a war. But nowadays it is quite easy for a very ordinary person to become a superstar. We only need to upload a remarkable video to the Internet, take part in a reality TV show, or make a controversial comment on a social media website for our names to be instantly recognized worldwide.

3 When you skim a text to find the main topic it will help you to identify words that are repeated or to find their synonyms (words that have similar meanings). For example, in the passage in Exercise 2, *person* is repeated twice and the word *figure* has a similar meaning.

4 Look at the passage again and underline other words and phrases that have similar meanings to each other.

Look at the groups of words and circle the one which does <u>not</u> have the same meaning as the rest.
a special   different   ordinary   unusual   outstanding
b renowned   unknown   prominent   famous   well-known
c big name   icon   idol   worker   hero
d debatable   questionable   arguable   contentious   acceptable
e local   global   international   universal   widespread

5 Another technique for identifying the main topic of a text is to read the first sentence of each paragraph. This is usually the topic sentence and summarizes the main points of the paragraph.

Read the following passage and choose the best title for it from the list below.
a Famous People in the Media
b The Press and Politics: an unhappy relationship
c Media and Celebrities: boundaries versus benefits
d The Dangers of Social Media
e Media and the Law

A Celebrities and the media have a distinctly 'love-hate' relationship and, whilst they recognize their mutual dependency, striking a balance between their respective interests is an on-going challenge for both groups.

B In the worlds of sport, entertainment and politics, celebrities depend on the press, social media, photographers and radio and television to raise their public profile, and afford them the visibility essential to success in their highly competitive professions. For example, top-class sports celebrities rely on income from commercial sponsorship to pay for expensive coaching, fitness and training facilities. In the entertainment business, glamorous award ceremonies and opening nights of much-anticipated films not only provide the cast with what is undoubtedly an enjoyable and well-deserved celebration of their success, but also an opportunity for valuable exposure to their fans as well as to influential figures in their own industry.

C At the same time, sales revenues from advertising and audience ratings are boosted by stories about famous figures, which range from casual gossip to carefully researched information, depending on their purpose and target audience.

D The conflict between these apparently compatible interests lies in deciding how much access the media should have to the daily lives of the famous and the amount of privacy any individual should be entitled to.

E This clash has been intensified in the first two decades of the 21st century by recent developments in communications and digital science. There can be little doubt that the dramatic expansion of online social media has made it possible to spread rumours, true or false, instantly across the globe. This has significantly increased the power of the press to enhance or damage the reputation of any public figure. Due to advances in high-tech photographic equipment, it has become easier than ever for photojournalists to intrude on the private lives of well-known personalities without their knowledge or agreement. This has led, on many occasions, to legal battles between the media and celebrities to determine whether newspapers should be entitled to publish images of high-profile personalities taken when they are not appearing in public. Another example of how the press has used dubious methods to obtain information about famous personalities is *phone hacking*, or listening in to private phone calls, which has also resulted in a number of court cases.

F In court, a judge may decide what the press is allowed to publish about well-known figures by taking 'public interest' into account. In this case, 'public interest' does not simply mean the number of people who would like to know more about the private lives of high-profile personalities, but how much society, as a whole, would benefit from this information.

Exam skills

Matching headings questions

In these questions you are asked to choose from a list of headings (numbered i, ii, iii, …) that refer to the main meaning of a paragraph or section of the text marked with letters (A, B, C, …). There will be more headings than there are paragraphs to match.

Skimming

To answer these questions you will need to find:

- the parts of the text that summarize the main idea of each paragraph or section.
- related or similar words in the headings (e.g., *famous figures*, *press*, *needs*, *conflicting*).

To identify the main idea of a paragraph you can skim the text, without looking for detailed information.

- Look for key topic words in the paragraph (e.g., *celebrities*, *media*).
- Find words that are repeated or connected with each other (e.g., *love*, *need*, *demands*, *hate*, *conflicting*).

6 Look at the reading passage and underline the key words in each paragraph.

7 Read the passage again and match each of the following headings with a paragraph.

Headings

i   The reputation of famous politicians
ii   The commercial advantages of reporting on celebrities
iii   The legal position
iv   Privacy and digital technology
v   All publicity is good publicity
vi   Conflicting demands of the press and famous figures
vii   Celebrities benefit from publicity
viii Fame versus privacy

Paragraphs

A _____vi_____

B _____

C _____

D _____

E _____

F _____

Exam skills

True/False/Not Given questions

This type of exam question asks you to decide whether a statement in the question:

- agrees with the information in the reading passage.
- does not agree with the information in the reading passage.
- is not mentioned in the reading passage.

Remember that your answer should be based only on the information in the text, not on what you already know. You can use the following technique to find the answers to True/False/Not Given questions.

1 Look for key words in the statement in the question.
2 Look for similar words or phrases in the passage to find the section that refers to the statement.
3 Decide whether the statement matches the information in the text.

Skills

Be very careful when you are checking to see whether information is <u>false</u> or <u>not given</u>.

- When the information is <u>not given</u>, you will <u>not find any information</u> about this topic in the reading passage.
- When the information is <u>false</u>, this may be indicated by a <u>negative, a comparative or a conditional</u> statement in the text.

    – Remember that not all negatives use a simple 'no', 'not' or 'nobody'. Expressions like *instead of, having failed to, without + [...ing]* can also indicate a negative.
    – False information may also be found in parts of the text that contain comparisons. Make sure you check these, *e.g., Screen celebrities are <u>less</u> likely to appear in the media than sports stars.*
    – Conditional sentences may also be indicators of false information. Compare the tenses of the verbs in the question statements with the verbs in the text to make sure they have the same meaning, e.g., *is/may be, can/could, saw/might have seen.*

8 Read the passage again and underline the words that are connected with the word *media*. Do not focus on other words.
    a Which words did you find?
    b What kinds of words (nouns, verbs, adjectives, adverbs) are they?
    c Think of alternative words or phrases for these words.

9 Statements 1–6 are taken from a True/False/Not Given task. Read the statements and underline the key words.
    a The needs of celebrities and the media do not conflict.
    b Film stars appear at film premieres to take advantage of the publicity.
    c Gossip about celebrities makes them successful.
    d Famous people have no right to any privacy.
    e Because technology has progressed, famous people have more difficulty protecting their privacy.
    f A large percentage of the population is interested in the private lives of public figures.

10 Look for phrases in the passage that have a similar meaning to the key words.

11 Decide whether the statements are True, False or Not Given.

Exam skills

Matching sentence endings

In this type of question you will be asked to match the first part of a sentence with a suitable ending, chosen from a list of possibilities. You will need to write the correct letter on your answer sheet. There will be more endings than sentences.

Skills

When you are looking for the correct ending for the sentence, you should look for:
- grammatical agreement – ask yourself if the ending is grammatically possible (e.g., Is the verb in the same tense? Do the subject and the verb agree? Is the sentence structure complete?).
- endings that cannot be correct because they are grammatically impossible.
- meaning – make sure that the second part of the sentence is on the same topic as the first part and check that it follows logically.

12 Read the sentence endings A–H from a Sentence matching question. Find the three endings that express purpose.

 A to support their training.
 B useful for helping actors find work.
 C based on research or just rumour.
 D disagree on the amount of privacy a person should have.
 E make it more difficult for famous figures to retain their privacy.
 F to obtain personal information.
 G considered in a legal case.
 H to give high-profile personalities publicity.

13 Look at the sentence beginnings a–g.

 i Which two beginnings are most likely to be followed by a phrase indicating purpose?
 ii Which two beginnings logically match the endings A–H in Exercise 12?

 a Technological developments
 b Reports in the press may be
 c Film premieres are
 d The press and celebrities sometimes
 e Famous sports personalities need sponsorship
 f Public interest may be
 g Phone hacking has often been used

14 Match each of the remaining sentence endings from Exercise 12 with a beginning from Exercise 13. Then skim the reading passage again to check your answers.

Reading Passage 1

You should spend 20 minutes on questions 1–14, which are based on Reading Passage 1.

Social Media Privacy: A Contradiction in Terms?

This article is by Naomi Troni, global CMO of Euro RSCG Worldwide.

A Never in the course of human interaction have so many shared so much about themselves with so many others — and with so little apparent concern for their privacy. Was it really just a generation ago that people kept all but their most basic information under virtual lock and key? Today, we happily share our date and place of birth, name of our first pet, mother's maiden name, favourite movie or book, favourite colour, first school teacher — and myriad other snippets of information required by online services as part of their security procedures.

B The basic premise behind this information-sharing is nothing new. Consumers have long handed over a little personal information in exchange for services such as banking and finance, utilities and healthcare. The big difference now is that the information is digitized and accessible online — and we're handing it out to virtually anyone who asks, regardless of how briefly the business has been in existence. Of even greater concern to many is the amount and variety of information being gathered about us *without* our explicit permission. Whereas retailers and others used to tweeze out information gleaned through loyalty cards, prize draws and catalogue mailing lists, now these old standbys have been massively augmented by customers researching and purchasing online, leaving in their wake a digital trail of cookie crumbs detailing their needs, tastes and desires.

C And then there's social media. If this isn't the Holy Grail* for marketers, it's difficult to imagine what would be. In this thoroughly 21st century communications channel, old notions of privacy simply do not apply; sharing personal information, experiences and opinions is the whole point of the service. And, wonder of wonders, consumers don't only provide it willingly — they provide it for free! Sure, some people take the precaution of limiting access to their Facebook or Google+ pages, but even these people typically are eager to share their thoughts via comment sections on news sites, reviews on retail sites and in branded clubs and forums.

D With all the time we spend online and all the forums we frequent, it's no wonder most of us have grown accustomed to doling out little snippets of personal information with barely a second thought. It helps that we rarely are asked to hand over a whole stack of personal information in one massive data transfer; that would be too much trouble and might provoke too much anxiety. Rather, we routinely hand it out a bit at a time.

E Anybody over the age of 30 likely will remember that in the early days of mainstream Internet, 10 to 15 years ago, consumers were wary about handing over private information. A 2001 UCLA report, for instance, found high levels of consumer concern over online privacy in general and credit card security in particular.

F Since then hundreds of millions of people have come online and become regular users of commerce sites and social media. Early concerns about online privacy have been sidelined by the desire for more speed, more convenience, more choice and more great deals. Familiarity has bred complacency and even foolhardiness; we've all heard about people uploading pretty much everything, including the most intimate words and images.

G Now, after a decade of consumers feeling increasingly free-and-easy with their personal information online, we are seeing signs of a new wariness setting in. In a Euro RSCG global survey conducted among 7,213 adults in 19 countries, we found that 55% of respondents are worried that 'technology is robbing us of our privacy'; the figure was above 60% in a number of countries, including the United States and China. Similarly, 61% overall agreed 'People share too much about their personal thoughts and experiences online; we need to go back to being more private.'

H And it's not just snooping companies and hackers that consumers fear. Nearly half the sample (47%) — and a majority of millennials* — worry that friends or family will share inappropriate personal information about them online. Around one-third overall already regret posting personal information about themselves.

* **Holy Grail** – a desired ambition or goal (in Christian tradition, the cup used by Jesus at the Last Supper with his followers)

* **Millennials** – people born between 1982 and 2000

Questions 1–5

*Reading Passage 1 has eight sections, A–H. Choose the correct heading for sections **B, C, D, F** and **G** from the list of headings below.*

*Write the correct number **i–vii** by question numbers 1–5.*

i   A reverse in trends

ii   Blogging

iii   Digital technology: a threat to privacy

iv   Privacy versus ease

v   Online social networks and consumer information

vi   Little by little

vii   Phone hacking and privacy

viii Attitudes at the turn of the century

Example: Paragraph E _____viii_____

1   Paragraph B   ....

2   Paragraph C   ....

3   Paragraph D   ....

4   Paragraph F   ....

5   Paragraph G   ....

Questions 6–10

Do the following statements agree with the information in the text?

By question numbers 6–10 write

    TRUE   *if the statement is true.*
    FALSE   *if the statement contradicts the information in the text.*
    NOT GIVEN *if there is no information about this.*

6 In the past, people shared their personal details freely.

7 Nowadays, individuals give their personal information to online services because it makes them feel safe.

8 Traditionally, financial organizations have asked their clients to provide a limited amount of information.

9 The difference between the past and the present is that private information is available digitally to a much larger number of people.

10 New businesses are not allowed to request personal information.

6 ....   **9** ....

7 ....   **10** ....

8 ....

Questions 11–14

*Complete each sentence with the correct ending **A–F** from the list below.*

*Write the correct letter **A–F** next to the question number.*

11 It is worrying that

12 Even people who protect their personal information on social networks

13 Online services ask for a small amount of information

14 Nearly 50% of people who responded to a survey about personal information

A there are strict controls on who has access to our personal details.

B did not trust people in their closest social networks to respect their privacy.

C because their customers would be worried about giving away a lot of information at one time.

D give away personal information on online forums and discussion boards.

E a lot of private information is gathered without our knowledge.

F to persuade users to provide them with details about their friends.

11 ....   **13** ....

12 ....   **14** ....

The 21st-century workplace

UNIT AIMS

READING SKILLS
Identifying different types of information
Scanning text for specific details

EXAM PRACTICE
Matching information in a text
Multiple-choice
Completing sentences

Answering multiple-choice questions

1 a When you are asked to look for specific information in a text, it helps to know what *kind* of information you want to find. For example, in a text describing the graph below, you would expect to find *numbers*, *percentages*, *dates* and *ratios*.

b What kind of information does the arrow indicate in this graph?

2 What kind of information would you find in the graphs and tables A–F below? Match the different types of information in the box with the images.

> tendencies ▪ ratios ▪ areas ▪ percentages ▪ eras ▪ schedules

A 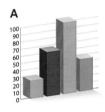 **B**  **C** **D** 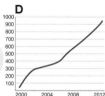 **E**  **F**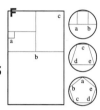

3 Look quickly over this block of text and find the following words and numbers: *proportion, Northumberland* and *1900*. Underline them, and then answer the questions below.

> juiperabtelegunerazeoirucremdebbatsNorthumberlandoemormmport
> mosl493waproportionstermeluquestasldinhaoloelbatskipszmxottrowet
> msuejid1900kwqjsdnndndhoo

Which ones could you see most easily? Choose the reason or reasons why.
The information:

- is in a bold font.
- is in the first line of the text.
- is in the middle of the text.
- starts with a capital letter.
- is a date.
- is a number.
- is a technical term.

Skills

Scanning for information

When you scan a text for specific information you do not need to read every word or line from left to right. Once you have decided what kind of information you want, you can let your eye move around the text and search for the features that are characteristic of that particular information. For example, you would look for *capital letters* for names of people and places, *symbols* and *numbers* for percentages, statistics and dates. Technical terms may be in *italics* or inverted commas ('...').

Computer Technology in the Workplace

A Although the earliest computers were developed in the United States during the first decades of the twentieth century, it was not until the beginning of the 1970s that computers (known as 'mainframe' computers) were used in industry and business. At this stage, however, computers were so large they needed a room of their own, and were not practical in the workplace.

B Nevertheless, soon afterwards, rapidly evolving technology produced smaller, more practical, desktop computers, which were developed commercially between the late 1970s and the mid-1980s. Despite this, it was only in the late 1980s that personal computers (PCs) became standard equipment in the workplace.

C Subsequently, and especially during the first 10 years of the 21st century, the concept of the workplace has been revolutionized. By creating *virtual environments*, technology has freed businesses from the restrictions of time and place. Thanks to sophisticated communication software, colleagues in countries as distant as Australia and the UK can talk to each other through their PCs, laptops, tablets and mobile phones, meeting almost as if they <u>were</u> in the same room and no longer limited to their physical location.

4 Answer the questions with information from the reading passage. Practise letting your eye skip over the text to search for particular words, numbers or groups of letters. For example, to find out <u>when</u> the events in the passage took place, focus on <u>dates</u> and <u>verb</u> tenses.

1 How many times are the 1980s mentioned in the passage?
2 How many references are there to time in the passage?
3 How many times does the word 'were' appear in the passage?
4 In which paragraph does the verb change to the present tense?
5 Why does the writer use 'were' again in paragraph C?

5 Scan the text again and complete the timeline with the letters A–E for each of the events in the list below. The first one has been done for you.

A mainframe computers utilized in commerce and manufacturing
B offices adopt widespread use of desktops
C online conferencing has broken down geographical barriers
D PCs widely available on the market
E initial developments in computer technology

E	___	___	___	___
1900–1960	1970–1975	1976–1985	1986–1989	present

6 Scan the text again and underline examples of other types of information from the list below.

place names ▪ periods of time ▪ technical terms

Exam skills

Matching information questions

In this type of exam question you will have to identify the paragraph or section of the passage that contains specific information. Before you answer the questions, decide what kind of information you are looking for.

7 Practice finding information in a section of the reading passage. The passage has three paragraphs, A–C. Which paragraph contains the information you need to answer the questions? Complete the table with the type of information and the paragraph where it can be found.

Question	Type of information	Paragraph
1 When were computers first used in industry?		
2 What were the early computers called?		
3 How does technology allow people in different countries to work together?		
4 What kind of technology has contributed to the expansion of the office beyond its geographical boundaries?		

Exam skills

Multiple-choice questions

In these exam questions you will have to choose the best answer from a list of alternatives provided and write the letter (A, B, C …) on your answer sheet. The number of alternative answers you have to choose can vary and you should read the question carefully to make sure you select the correct number. You may be asked to select:

• ONE answer out of FOUR alternatives
• TWO answers out of FIVE alternatives
• THREE answers out of SEVEN alternatives

Skills

When you are asked to select the correct answer from a list of alternatives, you can use the following techniques:

a Skim the alternatives quickly to identify any that are not possible. Remember, they may be on a different topic, or contain incorrect data.
b Decide which alternatives are grammatically possible.
c Compare the meaning of the grammatically correct alternatives with the sentences in the passage.
d Look for words or phrases in the statements that match or have a similar meaning to the words in the alternative answers.

8 Practice scanning for words that do not refer to the topic of the text. Underline the word in each list that does not relate to the same topic as the other three.

1 contest   employment   manufacturer   labour
2 communication   aspect   announcement   broadcast
3 advance   evolution   progress   provision
4 economy   routine   competition   cost
5 global   rights   worldwide   universal

9 Read the following text. Questions 1–4 are taken from a multiple-choice task that asks you to complete a sentence. You must choose ONE correct alternative out of FOUR.

1 Equal gender rights
 A are the result of globalization.
 B have been influenced by communication technology.
 C are one of the causes of new approaches to work.
 D have affected the global economy.

2 Workers in India work
 A in call centres.
 B longer hours than they did in the past.
 C standard office hours from 9–5.
 D for lower salaries than workers in other countries.

3 Communication technology has
 A improved working conditions in the office.
 B eliminated the need for business meetings.
 C expanded the boundaries of the workplace.
 D increased the cost of business trips.

4 Flexible working hours
 A are the result of women's dual roles.
 B have reduced the number of working mothers.
 C were introduced in 2003.
 D are a legal right for all employees.

A Over the past 30 years, both employer and employee attitudes to work and working patterns have been shifting. For many forward-looking companies, the office is no longer perceived as an indispensable base for work and business, and the effectiveness of the traditional 9–5 working day is increasingly being challenged.

B Three factors that have affected attitudes towards the working day and the ways in which workers interact with each other are: the globalization of the economy, widespread developments in communication technology and the expansion of equal opportunities for women.

C As a result of the globalized economy, there is intense competition for trade and service provision throughout the world. More than ever, workers in both developed and developing nations are recognizing the inevitable changes in their working environment, as they come into direct competition with each other for employment opportunities. An example of this is the growth of call centres in countries such as India, where technology is advanced, but the cost of labour comparatively cheap. Employees in these centres, working unsocial hours, routinely provide telephone support to callers in time zones far from their own. The growth of these 'timeless workplaces' has been made possible by other factors affecting perceptions of the office, the evolution of online communication software and the proliferation of wireless and mobile networks across the globe.

D One of the more obvious consequences of these technological advances is that businesses in distant countries can discuss and complete deals over the Internet, through online conferencing software, without the need for international travel. Additionally, as these conferences can be held not only in the office but anywhere – at home, in a coffee shop or in an airport – the concept of the office as a unique centre for work has been brought into question.

E Whilst the global economy and technological advances can account for some of the changing perceptions of the workplace, another contributing factor, is social innovation, particularly with regard to equal rights for women. Although large numbers of women have been employed in business and industry over the last century, they have also continued to be responsible for childcare and running the home. For this reason, they have traditionally worked part-time and have often needed to adapt their working hours to the demands of the family. To support this working pattern, a new law was passed in the UK in 2003, giving women with young children the right to request flexible working hours. Since then, further changes in equal rights legislation, allowing both men and women with families to apply for flexitime, have encouraged a widespread revision of attitudes to the workplace.

10 Look at the reading passage again. Questions 1–4 are taken from a different type of multiple-choice task. In this type of question, you must choose TWO correct alternatives out of FIVE.

Before you answer:

a Read the question.
b Find the paragraph in the reading passage that refers to the topic of the question.
c Read the alternatives.
d Delete any alternatives that are not possible.
e Choose the TWO correct alternatives.

1 What do innovative employers think about modern working styles?
   A Working patterns are 30 years out of date.
   B Workers' opinions about employers have changed recently.
   C The workplace has become less important as a centre of operations.
   D The office is an essential part of their business.
   E The standard eight-hour day is not as beneficial as it used to be.

2 Why do employees have to compete for work internationally?
   A Opportunities for work have decreased in developing countries.
   B Technological advances and low wages have made some countries more competitive than others.
   C The worldwide economic climate has affected the labour market.
   D People in India are prepared to work long hours in call centres.
   E Wireless networks have extended throughout the world.

3 How have developments in technology affected the workplace?
   A They have expanded the boundaries of the office.
   B The office has become more important as a place to meet clients.
   C Personal meetings have become more significant.
   D People have the option to work from different locations.
   E They have encouraged international travel.

4 How has legislation in Britain supported families?
   A It has reduced working hours for parents.
   B It has given parents the right to ask for flexitime.
   C It has given women the right to work part-time.
   D It allows fathers to spend more time with their children.
   E It has made women work fewer hours.

Reading Passage 2

You should spend 20 minutes on questions 1–12, which are based on Reading Passage 2.

A For years, employers have been aware of employee engagement* and retention issues in their workplaces. These organizations have engagement policies that typically address engagement for the organization under one policy, without any differentiation for the generations of employees. As the millennial generation (also commonly known as Gen-Y and includes births from 1982–2000) grows in the workforce and *baby boomers** retire, managers and human resources professionals will need to develop new engagement models that take into account the generational differences between baby boomers and millennials. In this article, I will highlight some of the characteristics that differentiate millennials from other generations and explain why employee engagement should be *top of mind* for managers.

B Baby boomers are currently the largest generation of active workers. Research has shown that boomers identify their strengths as organizational memory*, optimism and their willingness to work long hours. This generation grew up working in organizations with large corporate hierarchies, rather than flat management structures and teamwork-based job roles.

C Millennials have a drastically different outlook on what they expect from their employment experience. Millennials are well educated, skilled in technology, very self-confident, able to multi-task and have plenty of energy. They have high expectations for themselves, and prefer to work in teams, rather than as individuals. Millennials seek challenges, yet work-life balance is of utmost importance to them. They do, however, realize that their need for social interaction, immediate results in their work and desire for speedy advancement may be seen as weaknesses by older colleagues.

D The millennial generation is the largest age group to emerge since the baby boom generation, and as this group grows into a significant proportion of the workforce over the next 20 years, employers will need to make major adjustments in their engagement models. Motivating, engaging and retaining people will never cease as managerial priorities, but employers will have to carefully consider what strategies they will use to cultivate and retain valuable millennial employees now and into the future.

E Millennials are creating a change in how work gets done, as they work more in teams and use more technology. Their social mindset, however, is also a significant factor. As Leigh Buchanon writes in *Meet the Millennials*, 'One of the characteristics of millennials, besides the fact that they are masters of digital communication, is that they are primed to do well by doing good. Almost 70 percent say that giving back and being civically engaged are their highest priorities.'

UNIT AIMS

READING SKILLS

Identifying key information and data in a text

Matching textual information with diagrams

Recognizing stages in a process

EXAM PRACTICE

Labelling a diagram

Completing a table

Completing a flowchart

1 The words in the following list can be associated with water and sanitation. How many alternatives, related to the same topic, can you think of for each word? What are the opposites for each of these alternatives?

  a clean   **b** scarcity   **c** consumption   **d** disease

Skills

Identifying key information and data in a text

a To identify the main topic and sub-topics in a reading passage, scan it for words that are repeated frequently. Also look for synonyms (words with the same meaning) or related words.

b To find key data, scan the text again for numbers and symbols that give factual and statistical information related to the topic and sub-topics.

c Read the words on either side of the key words carefully to identify trends, negatives or comparisons.

2 Scan the following passage and underline the main topic and two sub-topics.

> For the inhabitants of nations where water is abundant and the processes for making it safe for human consumption well established, clean water may not seem an urgent issue. But in countries where water and the funds for converting it into drinking water are scarce, water quality is a matter of life and death. According to the World Health Organization (WHO), over a billion people live in parts of the world where there is simply not enough water. This forces them to drink water from unhygienic sources and risk contracting water-borne diseases.

3 Find facts and statistics in the passage below about water and sanitation. Complete the table with numbers and words from the text.

	1 _____ water	domestic water supply	adequate sanitation
world population	83%	2 _____ %	
developing countries			3 _____ %
South Asia/ sub-Saharan Africa			4 _____ %

Over the last 10 years there have been positive developments in the supply of safe water throughout the world. For example, World Health Organization figures show that 83% of the world's population has access to water from sources that have been treated to make it suitable for drinking. Statistics also indicate that over 50% of the population has water piped directly to their home.

On the other hand, some 2.6 billion people, half the population of the developing nations, do not have access to drainage or sanitation. Figures for South Asia and sub-Saharan Africa show that only around 30% of the population benefits from an acceptable level of sanitation.

4 Read the passage below and label the graph with no more than TWO WORDS from the text for each question.

In the 20 years between 1990 and 2010, there was a clear improvement worldwide in the provision of safe water for consumption. By 2010 the percentage of homes with a piped supply of water had risen to 54%, and the availability of treated water had increased by 4% since 1990 to 35% of the world's population in 2010. At the same time, the proportion of the world's population still using surface water for drinking reached an unprecedented low of 3%, whilst the percentage of the population using untreated water for drinking fell to 8%.

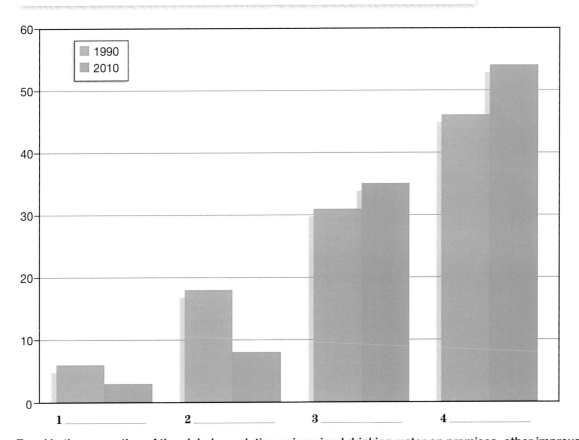

Trend in the proportion of the global population using piped drinking water on premises, other improved drinking water sources, unimproved sources and surface water, 1990–2010. (UNICEF JMP report 2012)

Exam skills

Diagram label completion

In this type of exam question you will have to label a diagram with words from a reading passage. The question will tell you exactly how many words you should use. Be careful not to use more words than the question requires, as you will lose marks. The answers to the questions may not be in the same order as the information in the text.

Skills

When you are asked to label a diagram from a text:

- look at the diagram and try to predict the kind of vocabulary you will need to complete the labels.
- scan the text for key words or numbers.
- match these with the diagram.

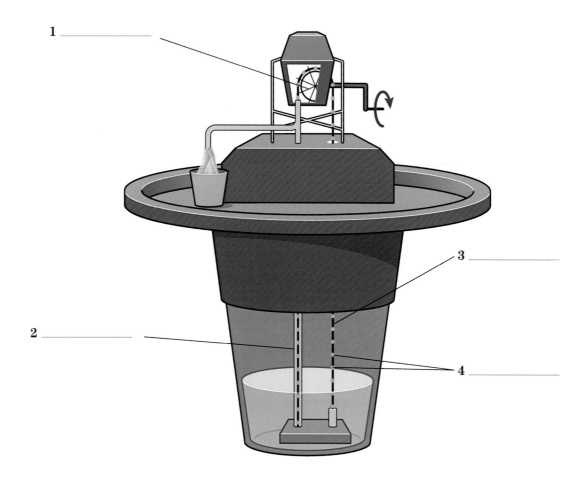

5 Look at the diagram and answer questions a and b.
   a What does the diagram show?
   b Which three key words would you expect to find in the description of this mechanism?

6 Complete the labels on the diagram with NO MORE THAN THREE WORDS for each blank space from the following reading passage.

> A water pump must be sustainable, which means it must be able to be fixed locally, cheaply and quickly. A rope pump is a simple technology that can be constructed from recycled parts like bicycle wheels, scrap metal and plastic.
>
> A long continuous loop of rope, with washers at regularly spaced intervals, runs around a wheel at the top of a well and around a smaller roller encased below the water line. The rope runs through a PVC pipe and, as the wheel is turned, water is drawn up the pipe by suction.

Skills

To identify the relative positions of different parts of a piece of machinery or equipment from a description, scan the text for prepositions.

7 Scan the reading passage again for prepositions and answer questions a–f.
   a Where are the washers?

   b Where is the large wheel?

   c Where is the small wheel?

   d Where does the rope pass around the wheel?

   e Where does the rope pass around the roller?

   f In what direction does the water move?

Unit 3

Exam skills

Flow chart completion

In one type of question you will be asked to complete a flow chart, usually a series of boxes connected by arrows which show a series of events. To prepare for this task, scan the text for words that indicate the relationship between one event and another, for example, words that express *sequence* or *condition* like: *first, second, then, after, before, finally, if, if not.*

8 Complete the flow chart about assessing water quality with NO MORE THAN TWO WORDS in each space from the reading passage that follows.

The selection of indicators and parameters for a programme of water quality assessment and analysis is likely to be country- (and possibly region-) specific and may also be specific to certain sources of water. Furthermore, the range of analysis and frequency of testing will be constrained by the resources available for water quality sampling and analysis and, whilst it may be desirable that a great number of indicators and parameters are analysed frequently, budget constraints may restrict the frequency of sampling and testing, or the number of indicators/parameters to be analysed. In general, however, there are some basic rules that should guide the development of water quality assessment programmes.

The first step in deciding whether a particular indicator/parameter should be included in the assessment programme is to make a judgment on the following critical questions:

- Is the contaminant or substance known to be present or absent in the waters of the country?
- If known to be present or if no information is available, then the indicator/parameter should be included. If it is known to be absent, then it should be excluded.
- If known to be present, at what concentration does the contaminant exist and does the concentration approach or reach levels which are of public health concern?
- What is the extent (temporal and spatial) of the presence of the contaminants?
- Are there any current or planned activities in catchment areas that may cause the contaminant to be present in water or levels to increase?

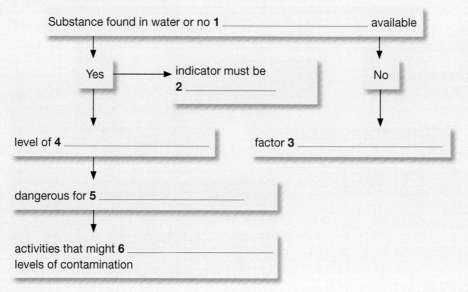

Reading Passage 3

You should spend 20 minutes on questions 1–12, which are based on Reading Passage 3.

The Millennium Development Goals

The MDG drinking water target has been reached. Over 2 billion people gained access to improved water sources from 1990 to 2010, and the proportion of the global population still using unimproved sources is estimated at only 11 per cent. This is less than half of the 24 per cent estimated for 1990. Almost 6.1 billion people, 89 per cent of the world's population, were using an improved water source in 2010. The drinking water target has thus become one of the first MDG targets to be met.

While this tremendous achievement should be applauded, a great deal of work remains.

First, huge disparities exist. While coverage of improved water supply sources is 90 per cent or more in Latin America and the Caribbean, Northern Africa and large parts of Asia, it is only 61 per cent in sub-Saharan Africa. Coverage in the developing world overall stands at 86 per cent, but it is only 63 per cent in countries designated as 'least developed'. Similar disparities are found within countries – between the rich and poor and between those living in rural and urban areas.

Second, complete information about drinking water safety is not available for global monitoring. Systematically testing the microbial and chemical quality of water at the national level in all countries is prohibitively expensive and logistically complicated; therefore, a proxy indicator for water quality was agreed upon for MDG monitoring. This proxy measures the proportion of the population using 'improved' drinking water sources, defined as those that, by the nature of their construction, are protected from outside contamination. However, some of these sources may not be adequately maintained and therefore may not actually provide 'safe' drinking water. As a result, it is likely that the number of people using safe water supplies has been over-estimated.

Finally, more than 780 million people remain unserved. Although the MDG drinking water target has been met, it only calls for halving the proportion of people without safe drinking water. More than one tenth of the global population still relied on unimproved drinking water sources in 2010.

Assessing progress towards the MDG target alone creates an incomplete picture, since countries that started out with low baseline coverage have had to work much harder to halve the proportion of the population without water and sanitation. Added to this is the challenge of rapid population growth, which can easily mean that any gains in people served are overtaken by population growth. Moreover, it is the poorest countries that are often characterized by a combination of low baseline coverage and high population growth. This means that countries may be making significant progress in the absolute number of people served, but still be persistently 'off track'.

In response, the JMP* has developed an alternative indicator that represents the proportion of the current population that has gained access over the period from 1995 to the most recent update, in this case 2010. It is thus the percentage of people living in a country today who have gained access in the last 15 years.

This indicator can be used to assess a country's performance irrespective of whether it started out with high or low baseline coverage. The indicator is expressed as: the increase since 1995 in the number of people with access as a proportion of the current (2010) population.

The graph shows selected countries in sub-Saharan Africa that have performed above the regional average of nearly 26 per cent. Some countries have made remarkable progress in providing large proportions of their population with access to improved drinking water sources, and this is true even of countries that are off track in terms of MDG progress. Rwanda and Sierra Leone, for instance, both experienced conflict during the period 1995 to 2010, but have nevertheless shown greater progress than that suggested by the regional average. In Rwanda, more than 30 per cent of the population have gained access to improved drinking water sources since 1995; this represents over 3 million people. Even countries that have not reported such good progress are noteworthy in terms of the number of people served.

The Democratic Republic of the Congo has provided improved water sources for only about 16 per cent of its population since 1995; still, this represents more than 10 million people. It is remarkable that sub-Saharan Africa has outstripped Eastern Asia in terms of the proportion of the current population that have gained access in the last 15 years.

* **JMP** – Joint Monitoring Programme

Questions 1–6

*Complete the table with information from Reading Passage 3. Write **NO MORE THAN TWO WORDS OR A NUMBER**.*

1990	2010
Projected percentage for 1990 **2** .... %.	11% of world's population using **1** ....
	3 .... % of global population using treated water.
	4 .... % of sub-Saharan population has access to safe drinking water.
	86% of population in **5** .... use improved water sources.
	63% have improved water in **6** .... countries.

Questions 7–10

*Complete the flow chart with information from Reading Passage 3. Select your answers from the list **A–F**.*

A drainage

B measurement

C unpolluted

D water sources

E inaccurate

F costly

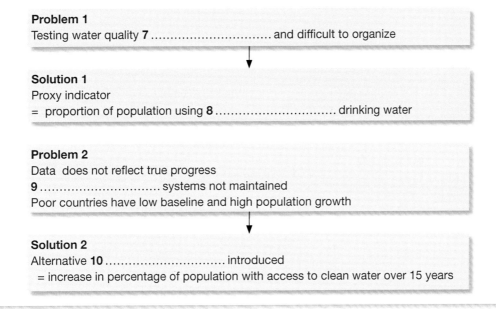

Problem 1
Testing water quality **7** .... and difficult to organize

↓

Solution 1
Proxy indicator
= proportion of population using **8** .... drinking water

Problem 2
Data does not reflect true progress
9 .... systems not maintained
Poor countries have low baseline and high population growth

↓

Solution 2
Alternative **10** .... introduced
= increase in percentage of population with access to clean water over 15 years

Questions 11–12

*Label the graph with information from Reading Passage 3. Write **NO MORE THAN FOUR WORDS AND/OR A NUMBER**.*

Percentage of population which has gained access to safe drinking water since 1995

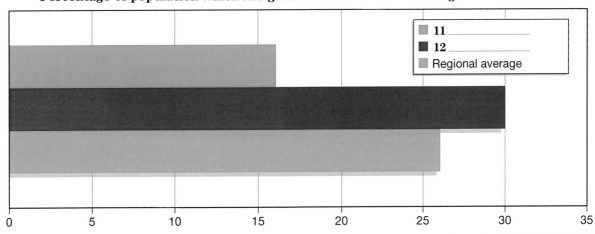

UNIT AIMS

READING SKILLS
Predicting main ideas from textual clues
Finding vocabulary for expressing
    opinions and ideas
Distinguishing between fact and opinion

EXAM PRACTICE
Matching headings
Multiple-choice
Yes/No/Not Given

A

B

Background knowledge of the topic

1 **a** What can you see in images A and B?

b What do you know about them?

Read the following headings and summarize each of them in two or three words. Try to predict what the main points of a paragraph with these headings might be.

1 Limited room for lift-off   3 Space – thrills or spills?
2 Wealthy tourists rocket into space   4 Fit for space?

2 Scan the following paragraphs and match them with headings 1–4 in Exercise 1.

A Spectacular views of planet Earth and its extraordinary oceans are one of the first attractions of space tourism. But do the dangers of space outstrip the risks of everyday air travel? While the majority of today's tourists accept that air travel is relatively safe, only a few specialist space travellers have, so far, needed to consider the greater hazards of journeying into the stratosphere.

B It is not difficult to imagine the physical demands a trip into space can make on the human body. During the ascent, the spaceship will travel at 3,500 miles an hour, producing powerful gravitational forces that affect the circulation of the blood. Aspiring space tourists will have to undergo rigorous medical examinations to ensure they are healthy enough to survive the voyage.

C Recent developments in space technology have quite literally widened horizons in the tourist market. But, the experience of voyaging further into space is likely to be limited to only the very prosperous. Reservations for flights into the stratosphere currently cost $200 000. After two days' training, the novice astronauts will embark on a journey that lasts less than an hour.

D The amount of fuel required to propel a spacecraft high into the stratosphere contributes significantly to the cost of travelling 100 kilometres up to the Karman line that marks the divide between Earth's atmosphere and space. One of the ways to reduce this is to impose strict controls on the weight of the space vehicle and restrict cabin space to an absolute minimum.

Skills

Predicting main ideas from textual clues

Written texts in English often (but not always) follow a predictable structure. For example, a text or paragraph may start with a general comment or background information on a topic, followed by more specific detail. The more general statement will outline the main idea of the text and the details will provide supporting information. This might take the form of a definition, an example or an explanation of the main topic. A typical paragraph may be organized in the following way: *general statement, example, explanation*; or *problem, example(s), cause(s), solution(s)*.

3 Number sentences a–d in the order you might expect to find them in a paragraph.

    a The aspiring space tourist will have to meet a number of criteria before being able to travel.

    b However, while the prospect of space tourism has become a fact, booking a ticket is not simple.

    c During the 21st century, space technology has developed to such an extent that space tourism has now become a reality.

    d First of all, as the price of a trip to the stratosphere is extraordinarily high, space tourists will have to be wealthy.

4 Match each sentence in Exercise 3 with a function i–v from the list below.

    i example   **ii** problem   **iii** solution   **iv** general statement   **v** explanation

5 Read the following passage about manned space travel. Look at paragraph C and compare the order of the sentences with your answers in Exercise 4. Were any of them different? If so, explain how you decided.

A In 1961, when the Russian astronaut, Yuri Gagarin, piloted the first manned space flight, space travel was still no more than a fantasy. All the same, long before space flight became a reality, Jules Verne and H. G. Wells had proposed creative solutions to some of its more obvious challenges, such as defying the force of gravity. In Verne's 1865 science fiction novel, *From the Earth to the Moon*, a group of Americans invented a huge cannon from which they planned to fire three men up to the Moon. In his 1901 novel, *First Men in the Moon*, Wells described a spaceship made of an imaginary gravity-defying material that would float up to the moon with its passengers inside.

B In the light of modern scientific knowledge, these early fictional scenarios seem absurd. But, it is important to recognize that during the late-19th and early-20th centuries the scientific study of space was more concerned with theoretical physics than the potential of manned space flight. Since the early 1960s, developments in space programmes and manned space flight have allowed over 500 people to travel into space. In fact, nowadays space travel has become such an everyday occurrence that the presence of a permanent, manned international space station in orbit round the Earth is no longer regarded as newsworthy.

C During the 21st century, space technology has developed to such an extent that space tourism has now become a reality. However, while the prospect of space tourism has become a fact, booking a ticket is not simple. The aspiring space tourist will have to meet a number of criteria before being able to travel. First of all, as the price of a trip to the stratosphere is extraordinarily high, space tourists will have to be wealthy. Secondly, the potential astronaut will have to be healthy. For example, because of the effect of the G-forces generated during lift-off, anyone suffering from a heart condition will not be eligible to fly. Space tourism will also be limited by ecological concerns, as the quantities of fuel required for each lift-off raise serious questions about environmental pollution.

D Despite these restrictions, as science progresses, space tourism is likely to become more popular in the future. For example, while developments in spacesuit design are expected to improve safety, technological advances in rocket design will probably reduce fuel consumption and, consequently, costs, making space travel accessible to a much larger proportion of the population.

Exam skills

Matching headings questions

In an exam question where you have to match headings with paragraphs, recognizing the structure of a reading passage can help you predict the possible order of the headings and identify them more easily.

6 Match paragraphs A–D with the functions on the list in Exercise 4.

7 Look at the reading passage again and match paragraphs A–D with headings i–vi. There are more headings than paragraphs.
   i   manned space flight over the years
   ii astronauts in fiction
   iii the future of space travel
   iv the profile of a space tourist
   v   future developments in space tourism
   vi the international space station

Exam skills

Multiple-choice questions

In one type of multiple-choice question you will have to select the correct answer from a list of possible options. Use the following technique to answer this type of question.
a Identify the topic by finding the key words in the question stem.
b Scan the text quickly to locate the key words.
c Read the section around the key words carefully and compare the meaning with the possible answers on the list.

8 Read the following passage and answer questions 1–5.

1 When did humans begin to study the universe?
   A During the 20th century.
   B When Copernicus was born.
   C A very long time ago.
   D When Newton discovered the law of gravity.

2 Why were large rockets important for radio communications?
   A They travelled long distances into outer space.
   B They could take direct measurements from the ionosphere.
   C They facilitated radio transmissions.
   D They helped scientists guess more about the ionosphere.

3 What did sounding rockets do?
   A They made a loud noise.
   B They carried astronauts into space.
   C They crashed on lift-off.
   D They gathered information at high altitudes.

4 Which of the following could rockets not do?
   A Launch a space capsule into orbit around the Earth.
   B Return a space probe from another planet.
   C Send a capsule into deep space.
   D Send a space probe to another planet.

5 When did the expression 'space science' become official?
   A When the Space Science Board was created.
   B When the media made it popular.
   C When rockets were invented.
   D Early in the history of space exploration.

Interest in the phenomena of space is not recent, its origins being lost in the shadows of antiquity. Impelled by curiosity and a desire to understand, man has long studied, charted and debated the mysteries of the celestial spheres. Out of this interest eventually came the revolution in thought and outlook initiated by Copernicus, supported by the remarkably precise measurements of Tycho Brahe, illuminated by the observations of Galileo and the insights of Kepler, and given a theoretical basis by Newton in his proposed law of gravitation. The Copernican revolution continues to unfold today in human thought and lies at the heart of modern astronomy and cosmology.

Yet, until recently, outer space was inaccessible to man, and whatever was learnt about the sun, planets and stars was obtained by often elaborate deductions from observations of the radiations that reached the surface of the Earth. Nor were all the inaccessible reaches of space far away. The ionosphere, important because of its role in radio communications, was not as far away from the man on the ground below as Baltimore is from Washington. Nevertheless, until the advent of the large rocket, the ionosphere remained inaccessible not only to man himself but even to his instruments. As a result many of the conclusions about the upper atmosphere and the space environment of the Earth were quite tentative, being based on highly indirect evidence and long chains of theoretical reasoning. Time and again the theorist found himself struggling with a plethora of possibilities that could be reduced in number only if it were possible to make in situ measurements. Lacking the measurements, the researcher was forced into guesswork and speculation.

Small wonder, then, that when large rockets appeared they were soon put to work carrying scientific instruments into the upper atmosphere for making the long-needed in situ measurements. From the very start it was clear that the large rocket brought with it numerous possibilities for aiding the investigation and exploration of the atmosphere and space. It could be instrumented to make measurements at high altitude and fired along a vertical or nearly vertical trajectory for the purpose, falling back to Earth after reaching a peak altitude. When so used the rocket became known as a sounding rocket or rocket sonde, and the operation was referred to as sounding the upper atmosphere.

A rocket could also be used to place an instrumented capsule into orbit around the Earth, where the instruments could make extended-duration measurements of the outer reaches of the Earth's atmosphere or observations of the sun and other celestial objects. Or the rocket might launch an instrumented capsule on a trajectory that would take it far from the Earth into what was referred to as deep space, perhaps to visit and make observations of the moon or another planet. The orbiting capsules were called artificial satellites of the Earth; those sent farther out came to be known as space probes or deep space probes. Finally, the ultimate possibility of carrying men away from the Earth to travel through deep space and someday to visit other planets emphasized dramatically the new power that men had acquired in the creation of the large rocket.

A language of rocketry emerged, which the news media popularized. Familiar words took on new meanings, and new terms were encountered: artificial satellite, spacecraft, space launch vehicle, rocket stages, countdown, lift-off, trajectory, orbit, tracking, telemetering, guidance and control, retrorockets, re-entry and space science.

Through all the centuries of scientific interest in space phenomena, the phrase space science had not gained common use. That the terminology did not come into use until after rockets and satellites brought it forth gives force to the definition of space science given at the start of this section. That definition sets forth the meaning in mind when in June 1957 the US National Academy of Sciences combined the functions of the IGY Technical Panel on Rocketry and the IGY Technical Panel on the Earth Satellite Program into a single board, naming it the Space Science Board.

Exam skills

Yes/No/Not Given questions

You may need to distinguish between two similar question types in the IELTS test.
- TRUE/FALSE/NOT GIVEN questions ask you decide whether the statements in the questions are correct, incorrect or not mentioned according to the <u>information</u> in the text.
- YES/NO/NOT GIVEN questions ask you to decide whether the statements in the questions agree or disagree with the author's <u>opinion</u> in the text.

In this type of question you will need to:
- distinguish between fact and opinion
- identify the writer's opinion

Skills

Identifying facts

Facts are often expressed with the verb *to be* and/or in the present or past simple.

For example, the following statements are usually accepted as facts: *Everest <u>is</u> the highest mountain in the world. The sun <u>sets</u> at 20.20 this evening. Light <u>travels</u> at 186 000 miles a second. Gravity <u>was discovered</u> by Isaac Newton.*

Identifying opinions

Opinions are expressed in a number of ways, for example in the use of:
- main verbs such as *claim, think, believe, argue.*
- modal verbs, such as *could, might, may.*
- adjectives, adverbs.
- words with negative connotations (*too, miss, impediment, trauma*).
- conditionals.

9 Read the following statements and decide whether they are facts or opinions.

   i Neil Armstrong made his 'one small step' on the Moon in 1969, only 12 years after Sputnik.
   _____

   ii Had the pace set by John F. Kennedy's Apollo programme been sustained there would already be footprints on Mars. _____

   iii Scientific exploration has burgeoned too. _____

   iv In coming decades, the entire solar system will be explored by flotillas of miniaturized unmanned craft. _____

   v The space shuttle failed twice in 135 launches. _____

Reading Passage 4

You should spend 20 minutes on questions 1–13, which are based on Reading Passage 4.

People who are alive today will walk on Mars

A Charles Bolden, NASA's administrator, averred that the robotic vehicle *Curiosity* will 'blaze a trail for human footprints on Mars'. He could be right. But there is a gulf between what is technically feasible and what is actually achieved.

B Neil Armstrong made his 'one small step' on the Moon in 1969, only 12 years after Sputnik. Had the pace set by John F. Kennedy's Apollo programme been sustained there would already be footprints on Mars. But that was driven by the urge to beat the Russians; there was no motive to sustain such huge expenditure.

C Scientific exploration has burgeoned too. In coming decades, the entire solar system will be explored by flotillas of miniaturized unmanned craft. Robots will mine raw materials from asteroids* and fabricate large structures. The Hubble Telescope's successors will further expand our cosmic vision of galaxies and nebulae*.

D But what role will humans play? There is no denying that *Curiosity* may miss startling discoveries no human geologist could overlook. But robotic techniques are advancing fast – whereas the cost gap between manned and unmanned missions remains huge.

E The main impediment to a manned NASA programme has always been that public and political opinion constrains it into being too risk-averse. The space shuttle failed twice in 135 launches. Although astronauts or test pilots would willingly accept this risk level, the shuttle had been promoted as safe for civilians. So each failure caused a national trauma and was followed by a hiatus in the programme while costly efforts were made – with very limited effect – to reduce the risk still further.

F Unless motivated by pure prestige, ambitious manned missions will be viable only if they are cut-price ventures, accepting high risks – perhaps even 'one-way tickets'. These may have to be privately funded; no Western government agency would expose civilians to such hazards.

G The SpaceX company, led by the entrepreneur Elon Musk, has successfully sent a payload* into orbit and docked with the Space Station. The involvement in space projects of Mr Musk and others in the high-tech community with credibility and resources is surely a positive step.

H Richard Branson will soon be lobbing people into space to experience a few minutes of weightlessness. Within a few years private companies will offer orbital flights. Maybe after another decade the really wealthy will be able to take a week-long trip around the far side of the Moon – voyaging farther from Earth than anyone has been before but avoiding the greater risks of a Moon landing and blast-off.

I The phrase 'space tourism' should, however, be avoided. It lulls people into believing that such ventures are routine and low-risk. If that becomes the perception, the inevitable accidents will be as traumatic as those of the space shuttle. Remember that nowhere in our solar system offers an environment as clement even as the Antarctic or the top of Everest. It is foolish to claim, as some do, that mass emigration into space offers escape from Earth's problems.

J But I believe, and hope, that some people living now will walk on Mars. Moreover, a century or two from now, small groups of intrepid adventurers may be living there or perhaps on asteroids quite independently from Earth. Whatever ethical constraints we impose here on the ground, we should surely wish such pioneers good luck in genetically modifying their progeny to adapt to alien environments.

K This might be the first step towards divergence into a new species: the beginning of the post-human era. And machines of human intelligence could spread still farther. Whether the long-range future lies with organic post-humans or intelligent machines is a matter for debate. Either way, dramatic cultural and technological evolution will continue not only here on Earth but far beyond.

* **asteroids** – tiny planets that orbit the Sun
* **nebulae** – clouds of gas between the stars
* **payload** – cargo of equipment

Questions 1–6

The reading passage has eleven paragraphs (A–K). Choose the correct headings for paragraphs C–H.

List of headings

i	Space travel for leisure
ii	Potential and reality
iii	Life after humans
iv	Transporting goods into space
v	Mechanized investigation
vi	Future colonies in outer space
vii	Commercial funding for dangerous ventures
viii	High-risk travel
ix	Avoiding disasters
x	Man versus machine
xi	The end of the race for space

Example: Paragraph A _____ii_____

1 Paragraph C   ....

2 Paragraph D   ....

3 Paragraph E   ....

4 Paragraph F   ....

5 Paragraph G   ....

6 Paragraph H   ....

Questions 7–10

Do the following statements agree with the claims of the writer in the passage?

Write

YES   if the statement agrees with the writer's claims.
NO   if the statement contradicts the writer's claims.
NOT GIVEN   if it is impossible to say what the writer thinks about this.

7   The Americans had no reason to continue spending large amounts of money on their space programme once they had won the race to the Moon.

8   One of the advantages of robots is that they notice unusual objects which human scientists might not see.

9   It would be wrong for future space explorers to alter their children's genes to make it possible for them to live on other planets.

10 Whatever the evolution of the species in the future, it should remain human.

Questions 11–13

Choose the correct letter (**A, B, C** or **D**) from the options in the list.

11 What will future unmanned spacecraft be able to do?

   A   Damage asteroids.

   B   Exploit new sources of materials.

   C   Travel beyond the solar system.

   D   Discover geological features that humans would not notice.

12 Why was the shuttle programme suspended?

   A   Because it was restricted to astronauts.

   B   Because it was safe for civilians.

   C   Because it was considered too dangerous.

   D   Because astronauts refused to take any more risks.

13 What is wrong with the expression 'space tourism'?

   A   It claims that it is dangerous to visit the Antarctic.

   B   It suggests that travelling into space is cheap.

   C   It should be avoided.

   D   It gives the impression that travelling into space is safe.

5 Sport
and sponsorship

UNIT AIMS

READING SKILLS
Finding organizational words
Recognizing relationships between ideas

EXAM PRACTICE
Identifying information (True/False/Not Given)
Matching information in factual texts
Matching features in texts

Thinking about the topic in advance

1 Look at the photos and answer the following questions.
  a   What sporting events can you see in the pictures?
  b   What other sports can you name?
  c   What are the most popular sports in your country?
  d   Why do you think people practise sports?
  e   Who sponsors sport?
  f   Why do you think they do this?

2 Match the following sports with the place where they are practised.
  Example: javelin – field

Sports		Locations	
i	athletics	a	court
ii	volleyball	b	field
iii	triple jump	c	track
iv	cycling	d	pitch
v	tennis	e	cross-country
vi	diving	f	slope
vii	gymnastics	g	mat
viii	orienteering	h	pool
ix	skiing		
x	football		

3 *Suffixes* are groups of letters that can be added to a word to change its form: -ist -er -ship -ion -ing -tic -ial

For example: play (v) + *er* → player (n)

Add suffixes from the list to the words below to form new words.

> sponsor ▪ athlete ▪ cycle ▪ dive ▪ promote ▪ finance ▪ fund

4 Complete the sentences with the words you formed in Exercise 3. There is one correct answer for each space.

   a The lead _____ in the Tour de France road race wears a yellow shirt.

   b Sportsmen frequently apply to large organizations for _____ support, to cover the cost of equipment and training.

   c _____ is an effective sales strategy to increase product _____ .

   d Olympic® _____ nowadays are required to compete from a 10-metre high platform.

   e The modern Olympics® originated from Greek _____ competitions which started nearly three thousand years ago.

Skills

Recognizing relationships between ideas

The ideas in a reading passage can be related in a number of ways. For example, linking phrases that indicate the relationship between events, or the logical progression of the writer's argument; organizational words that connect different sections of the passage. Events and ideas are often connected by words and phrases that indicate:

i   Chronological progression
ii Sequence in a process
iii Cause and effect
iv Contrast or comparison
v   Condition or concession

Another way of linking ideas is to use words that refer to information previously given or information to be given later in the text. Words like *this*, *that*, *these*, *those*, *who*, *which* and *it* are often used in this way.

5 Scan the following paragraphs and underline the words or phrases that connect the main ideas.

A Historical records show that the Olympic Games® were first staged as early as 776 BC on the plains of Olympia in ancient Greece. Afterwards, the games took place every four years for over a thousand years, until 393 AD, when they were prohibited by the Roman Emperor Theodosius. Fifteen hundred years later, in 1896,
5   the first modern summer Olympics® were held in Athens and have continued ever since, having been cancelled on only three occasions, during the First and Second World Wars.

B Before *they* can apply to the International Olympic® Committee to host the Olympic Games®, cities must be approved by their National Olympic® Committee. Following
10 *this*, they take part in a selection process consisting of two stages. The first phase is called the 'Applicant' phase, during *which*, each city's application is examined to consider whether *it* is adequately prepared and has the potential to organize the Olympic Games®. Only cities which fulfil *these criteria* continue to the second phase of bidding, known as the 'Candidate' phase.

15 **C** Because the Olympic Games® are primarily sporting events, it is possible to forget that they are also huge commercial ventures. In each country the impact of the Olympic Games® on the economy, infrastructure and environment of the host city depends on the national Olympic® committee's approach to planning for the

future. For example, one of the most important consequences of the 2012 Olympic
20   Games® in London, was the implementation of a regeneration plan for the east of
the city, which will result in improved social and housing facilities for local residents.

D Not everybody knows that there are two Olympic Games®; the more famous one
in the summer and the other in the winter, two years later. The summer and winter
Games differ in a number of ways. For instance, because the winter Games are
25   limited to events that require snow and ice, the summer Olympics® stage a wider
range of sports. As well as this, the winter Games are inevitably held in colder
climates and receive fewer visitors. However, many people say they prefer the winter
Olympics® because they find the skiing, bobsleighing and ice-skating more exciting
than the traditional athletic contests of the summer games.

30   **E** It is widely understood that the main aim of any sporting team is to play as well
as possible and win every game. But what happens if an Olympic® team loses
deliberately? Unless an Olympic® team genuinely tries to defeat its competitors, it is
considered to be 'not using its best efforts to win a match'. Whenever this happens,
the team is disqualified from the competition.

6 Read paragraph B again. What do the following words refer to in the passage?
  a *they* (line 8)
  b *this* (line 10)
  c *which* (line 11)
  d *it* (line 12)
  e *these criteria* (line 13)

Exam skills

True/False/Not Given

In this type of question, remember to answer according to the information in the text. If the
information in the question is clearly incorrect, you should answer FALSE. If it <u>could be</u> correct,
but is not explicitly mentioned, you should answer NOT GIVEN.

7 Without reading the text about the Super Bowl, read the following statements and write T on the
line after each statement that <u>could be</u> correct and F if the statement <u>could not</u> possibly be true.

  i 100% of American households watch the Super Bowl games. _____

  ii Super Bowl audiences are unusual because they pay special attention to the
  advertisements. _____

  iii A quarter of the products promoted during the Super Bowl in 2009, were also on YouTube.
  _____

  iv Half a minute of advertising during the 2008 Super Bowl cost $3 million. _____

  v Apple® commercials are more innovative than other Super Bowl advertisements. _____

8 Now read the passage about the Super Bowl and check whether the statements i–v are True, False or Not Given, according to the information in the text.

A The significance of the Super Bowl as an advertising vehicle is well recognized in US advertising practice. The US advertising industry has traditionally focused on Super Bowl telecasts because of the tremendous size of audiences and the outstanding rating points they receive. In recent years, Super Bowl telecasts have reached over 90 million viewers and more than 40% of US households (Kaplan, 2007; Steinberg, 2008a; Yelkur et al, 2004). In addition, there is a tendency for Super Bowl audiences to behave in a very specific way that is attractive to advertisers and provides them with very unique and valuable opportunities. That is, Super Bowl viewers tend to turn off their laptops, cell phones, digital recorders, etc. specifically to 'watch' not only the game, but also the new commercials that they will then talk about afterwards (Gunter and Furnham, 1997; Jensen, 1998; Mohr, 2007; Poole, 2007).

B More recently, the attractiveness of running ads during the Super Bowl has been found in cyberspace too. According to a Google executive, about 90% of brands advertising on TV during the 2009 Super Bowl also had ads up on YouTube. A quarter also tapped social networks to try and drive up additional comments, ratings and conversation (Klaassen, 2009). There is a trend for Super Bowl ads to draw significant amounts of online traffic to advertisers' branded websites. Anheuser-Busch found that traffic to its branded websites rose by 600 per cent, or 21 million views, in the seven days following its Super Bowl ads in 2008 (Mullman, Steinberg, Halliday, Zmuda and Parekh, 2009). For these reasons, obtaining spots during the Super Bowl telecast has become a competition in and of itself. In 2009, companies were willing to invest $3 million for a 30-second commercial spot (Futterman and Vranica, 2008).

C Although the Super Bowl serves as an advertising vehicle for many companies, very little is known about the creative strategies these companies employ to promote their products and services in Super Bowl commercials. This is rather surprising, given that Super Bowl advertising is considered cutting-edge from a creative perspective. For example, Apple Computer's '1984' ad, which introduced the Macintosh personal computer in a George Orwell-style, is considered one of the greatest commercials of all time in the US (Horton, 1990). Nonetheless, only a few studies have examined the creative strategies of Super Bowl commercials.

Unit 5

Exam skills

Matching information questions

In this type of question you will have to find detailed information in a specific section of a reading passage. You will be asked to write the letter that refers to the paragraph in the text where you have found the information. Sometimes you may find more than one piece of information in the same section, so you may need to use the same letter more than once.

9 The reading passage has three paragraphs, labelled A–C. Which paragraphs contain the following information? Choose the correct letter A–C. NB You may use any letter more than once.

    i   Why marketing firms are particularly interested in the people who watch Super Bowl games.

    ii The percentage increase in visits to a commercial website after a Super Bowl ad.

    iii Research about techniques for designing Super Bowl advertisements.

    iv Reasons why the Super Bowl is an effective means of marketing.

    v   The impact of Super Bowl commercials on online advertising.

Skills

Grouping and classifying information are important reading skills, which involve recognizing the qualities or features that define groups or the characteristics that link events.

10 Match the following items with the categories A–C. Write the correct letter by each number.

        A types of sport
        B sporting events
        C types of sponsorship

    i   equestrian
    ii   grant
    iii   FIFA World Cup^{TM} football
    iv   gymnastics
    v   endorsement
    vi   Winter Paralympics
    vii   subsidy
    viii patronage
    ix   Wimbledon Tennis Championships
    x   aquatic

Exam skills

Matching features

In some questions you will be asked to match the statements in the questions to a group of features from a lettered list. Do not expect the statements to match exactly with the options. Some of the options may not be used and others may be used more than once.

Reading Passage 5

You should spend 20 minutes on questions 1–14, which are based on Reading Passage 5.

A The recent global economic shift away from state-regulated economies and towards privatization has affected many areas of society. The sporting world is no exception to this, and football is a prime example. In fact, it can be argued that over the last 10 years, football clubs have become more focused on the commercial opportunities presented by international and league cup events than on their players' sporting prowess. In addition to this, football has become so powerful an economic force in some countries that its impact can be observed in political and government circles.

B Over the years, football clubs have transcended their original function. No longer supporting their teams solely through membership contributions, they have transformed themselves into a highly lucrative industry. This change in the financial sponsorship model of professional football has been described by Andreff (2000) as a shift from the 'Spectators – Subsidies – Sponsors – Local' model, which was prevalent in the 1970s, to the 'Media – Magnates – Merchandising – Markets – Global' paradigm, which emerged in the 1980s.

C Over the last 30 years, the growth of the broadcasting industry, and in particular its effectiveness as a channel for marketing and advertising, has increased the commercial profitability of football at national and international levels. This in turn has attracted a wide range of private investors, including individual billionaires, multi-national media companies, sports equipment suppliers and health product manufacturers. Some, but not all, of these are driven purely by an interest in monetary gain. Others are genuine fans, in the original sense of the word; that is, they are fanatical about football, investing in the game to satisfy their passion.

D In order to maximize their profits, more commercially motivated investors have extended their interests beyond the boundaries of receiving income from ticket sales. Branding, which has become a highly successful income stream in the last few decades, is an example of this. Products of all kinds, ranging from clothing to tableware and from mascots to sports equipment are manufactured in factories in various countries and distributed through high street commercial outlets worldwide. For example, a T-shirt or a mug branded with the logo of a European premier league football club may be produced on a continent as far away as Asia. A further, and even more productive, source of income is the sale of broadcasting rights. For example, in 2010, the governing body of world football (FIFA), earned 2408 million US dollars from the sale of the television rights to the FIFA World Cup™ in South Africa and 1072 million US dollars in marketing rights. Another profitable, but arguably dubious, commercial operation is the transfer of players from one football club to another. Although individual players receive astronomical fees as a result of these transfers, it is difficult to view the process as being very different from that of trading manufactured goods.

E As well as raising specific ethical issues, the transfer of players for large sums of money highlights the tension between the social ideals on which many sporting associations are founded and commercial necessity. Although many sports clubs may still retain their original social aims, such as health, social interaction and physical development, the financial pressures of the modern competitive world of international business prevent them from attaining these aspirations.

F These concerns were echoed some years ago by Bayle and Durand (in Rouvrais-Charron and Durand, 2009) who noted 'a growing gap between ethics and behaviour' amongst the governing bodies of international sport. It must be recognized that the challenge of balancing ideology, social responsibility and commercial viability is not unique to football. Nevertheless, it could be argued that if sport (and in this case, football) is based on the principle that it has a uniquely social function, this conflict between ideology and commercial pressure may be felt to be all the more acute.

Questions 1–6

*The reading passage has six paragraphs (**A–F**). Which paragraphs contain the following information?*

1 different modes of sponsorship

2 the range of organizations that invest in football

3 reasons for investing in football

4 the development of football from a sport to an industry

5 examples of promotional goods

6 a change in the status of footballers

Questions 7–10

Do the following statements agree with the information given in the passage?

Write

TRUE	*if the statement agrees with the information in the passage.*
FALSE	*if the statement disagrees with the information in the passage.*
NOT GIVEN	*if the information is not mentioned in the passage.*

7 In the past, football was not a commercial venture.

8 FIFA earned more from marketing than from broadcasting rights to the FIFA World Cup™ in South Africa.

9 Sporting associations believe that they have a social responsibility.

10 Commercially motivated sponsors are not concerned with ethics.

Questions 11–14

*Look at the following items (Questions 11–14) and the list of groups below. Match each item with the correct group. Write the letter **A–C**.*

NB *You may use any letter more than once.*

> **A**   football clubs
> **B**   sponsors
> **C**   the players

11   They use sport as a marketing tool.

12   They are becoming more controlled by private industry.

13   They are politically powerful.

14   They have been converted into merchandise.

6

Families

UNIT AIMS

READING SKILLS
Identifying main ideas
Identifying supporting ideas

EXAM PRACTICE
Multiple-choice questions
Completing sentences
Matching sentence endings

Predicting main ideas

1 Look at the photos and answer the following questions.
  a What can you see in the images?
  b What kind of information would you expect to find in an article about each of the photos?
  c Suggest a heading for an article about each photo.
  d What do you think the most important points of each article might be?
  e What kind of detail might support these points?

Skills

Identifying main ideas and supporting ideas

It is important to recognize the main idea in a paragraph and to distinguish it from the supporting ideas. Most paragraphs (but not all) start with a *topic sentence* that outlines the main theme of the paragraph. When the topic sentence is not the first sentence in the paragraph, you will need to read the text more carefully to find a sentence that gives a broad picture of the theme. Supporting ideas are often examples or explanations of the main idea.

2 Read the following sentences and decide whether they are likely to be main points or supporting points in a paragraph. Write *M* or *S* after each sentence.

Paragraph A

1 In early agricultural and hunting communities the social structure tended to be based on a tribal rather than a family pattern. ————

2 Although the family is the most common social grouping, it is not the only type of social organization. ————

3 One of the advantages of the tribal structure is that children can be cared for by a wide group of adults, thus increasing the community's prospects of survival and continuation. ————

4 This is still the case in social groups like the Amazonian and African tribes that maintain their traditional lifestyles. ————

Paragraph B

1 A case in point would be the one-parent, adoptive family, a relatively new category, resulting from recent changes in criteria for adoption. ————

2 Extended, nuclear and single-parent families are defined by their size, whereas foster and adoptive families are identified by their functions. ————

3 Families can be classified in a number ways, for example, by size or function or the origin of family members. ————

4 Furthermore, when a family fits into more than one category it creates a new classification. ————

5 Migrant and mixed-race families, on the other hand, are examples of families that are described by the racial or national origin of their members. ————

Paragraph C

1 This system allows the whole group to benefit from the experience of the older members of the family as well as the physical strength of their children and grandchildren. ————

2 Family structures across the world are determined by local culture, tradition and national economy. ————

3 By contrast, in urban populations, where space is limited and the cost of living higher, the nuclear family tends to be in the majority. ————

4 For instance, farming communities traditionally depend on the extended family to work on the land, sowing, harvesting and processing the crops. ————

3 Write the number of each sentence in Exercise 2 in the order you would expect to find them in a paragraph.

A: ———— , ———— , ———— , ————

B: ———— , ———— , ———— , ———— , ————

C: ———— , ———— , ———— , ————

4 Compare the following paragraphs with your answers in Exercise 3. If the sentence order is different in your answers, explain how you decided.

Paragraph A
Although the family is the most common social grouping, it is not the only type of social organization. In early agricultural and hunting communities the social structure tended to be based on a tribal rather than a family pattern. This is still the case in social groups like the Amazonian and African tribes that maintain their traditional lifestyles. One of the advantages of the tribal structure is that children can be cared for by a wide group of adults, thus increasing the community's prospects of survival and continuation.

Paragraph B
Families can be classified in a number of ways, for example, by their size or function or the origin of the family members. Extended, nuclear and single-parent families are defined by their size, whereas foster and adoptive families are identified by their functions. Migrant and mixed-race families, on the other hand, are examples of families that are described by the racial or national origin of their members. Furthermore, when a family fits into more than one category it creates a new classification. A case in point would be the one-parent, adoptive family, a relatively new category, resulting from recent changes in criteria for adoption.

Paragraph C
Family structures across the world are determined by local culture, tradition and national economy. For instance, farming communities traditionally depend on the extended family to work on the land, sowing, harvesting and processing the crops. This system allows the whole group to benefit from the experience of the older members of the family as well as the physical strength of their children and grandchildren. By contrast, in urban populations, where space is limited and the cost of living higher, the nuclear family tends to be in the majority.

Exam skills

Multiple-choice questions

In multiple-choice questions that ask you to complete a sentence from a list of options, remember to check that the match is grammatically possible.

5 Read the following passage and select TWO correct answers from the FIVE options (A–E).

1 Immigrant parents
   A belong to the local community.
   B feel isolated from the majority of society.
   C are bilingual.
   D learn to speak a second language.
   E are financially successful.

2 Learning the language of the host community
   A increases the possibility of integrating with the majority group.
   B guarantees well-paid employment.
   C increases employment opportunities.
   D improves the children's educational performance.
   E reduces family tensions.

3 The writer believes that immigrant parents
   A do not have deliberate language policies.
   B understand the advantages of bilingualism.
   C do not want to remember their past.
   D accept that they will lose touch with their children.
   E want to share their cultural background with their children.

It is widely documented that immigrant parents, who are typically members of minority groups, may experience stress, alienation, discrimination or inherent gaps with the majority group and find themselves raising children in the context of more than one language. Parents in these groups often attribute their decision or efforts to encourage L2* acquisition for themselves as well as for their children (parallel to L1* maintenance) to the potential economic benefits of bilingualism (e.g., Curdt-Christiansen, 2009; Guardado, 2008; King and Fogle, 2006), emphasizing the advantages of being absorbed into the wider society and the necessity of mastering the majority language for the sake of better work prospects in the future. This pattern can serve as an example of a coping mechanism. It is an explicit opinion frequently leading to an explicit decision, which protects family members (mainly the parents) from psychological disequilibrium. They consciously and purposefully decide to promote bilingualism in the family, pointing to its benefits and strengthening themselves as a system.

Another common finding when exploring FLP* is the insistence on language maintenance so as to facilitate the children's communication with members of the extended family, to promote family cohesion and to enable free and spontaneous communication between parents and children (e.g., Pavlenko, 2004; Smolicz et al, 2001; Tannenbaum, 2005; Tannenbaum and Howie, 2002). This too is an instance of a coping mechanism, since it involves explicit, conscious ideas about language and family dynamics to increase adaptiveness. It could also, however, be a defensive one. Many immigrants are not aware that, by promoting language maintenance, they are applying defensive strategies that often serve to protect the integrity of the family system ... These strategies involve, *inter alia*, maintaining strong emotional contact with the past, with childhood memories, parents and grandparents via language maintenance; or witnessing children developing competency in the parental language, which in turn may lead to further identification with the children, and/or prevent alienation and remoteness when children develop mastery only in L2; or maintaining symbolic links with the parental heritage.

* **L2** – second language
* **L1** – first language, native language, mother tongue
* **FLP** – family language policy

Exam skills

Sentence completion questions

This type of question requires you to complete a sentence with a certain number of words taken from the reading text. You do not need to change the words or write your own. Remember to use the exact number of words given in the question. You will lose marks if you use more.

6 Read the passage again and complete the sentences with ONE WORD from the passage.

1 Immigrant families frequently learn the language of their adopted country in order to take full advantage of their potentially improved _____ situation.

2 The family's decision to integrate with the host country is a means of preventing _____ instability.

3 The children of many migrant families maintain effective _____ with the older generation by continuing to speak their native language.

4 First language maintenance can be seen both as a coping and a _____ mechanism.

5 By continuing to use their mother tongue, immigrants can strengthen their children's _____ with their cultural background.

Exam skills

Matching sentence endings

In this type of question you will be asked to match the beginning of a sentence with an ending. There are more optional endings than beginnings and the questions are in the same order as the information in the text.

Skills

7 Before you select a sentence ending, look carefully at the:
- subject-verb agreement.
- verb tense.
- possible meaning of each part of the statement.

Match the beginning of each sentence (A–E) with the correct ending (i–vii).

A The relationship between the younger and older members of the family
B The number of households in the UK containing more than one family
C When marriage was more common, the number of children living with a single parent in the UK
D In 1996, 73 per cent of dependent children
E Since 1996, there

i were unusual.
ii is influenced by the size of the family.
iii has risen noticeably in the last 15 years.
iv was lower.
v has been an increase in the number of single-parent households.
vi have been improving in recent years.
vii were living with a married couple.

Reading Passage 6

You should spend 20 minutes on questions 1–13, which are based on Reading Passage 6.

Parental roles

One of the most enduring elements of social and behavioural science research in the last half of the 20th century was the scholarly re-examination of traditional ideas about fatherhood and motherhood. For over 200 years maternal behaviour had been considered paramount in child development (Kagan, 1978; Stearns, 1991; Stendler, 1950; Sunley, 1955), and fathers were often thought to be peripheral to the job of parenting because children throughout the world spent most of their time with their mothers (Fagot, 1995; Harris, Furstenberg and Marmer, 1998; Munroe and Munroe, 1994). Some argued that fathers contributed little to children's development except for their economic contributions (Amato, 1998), and others believed that fathers are not genetically endowed for parenting (Belsky, 1998; Benson, 1968). Indeed, even though Margaret Mead concluded that fathers were important contributors to childcare, and that '(a)nthropological evidence gives no support ... to the value of such an accentuation of the tie between mother and child' (Mead, 1956, pp.642–643), Mead (1949) perceived basic differences between fathers and mothers. The mother's nurturing tie to her child is apparently so deeply rooted in the actual biological conditions of conception and gestation, birth and suckling, that only fairly complicated social arrangements can break it down entirely ... But the evidence suggests that we should phrase the matter differently for men and women – that men have to learn to want to provide for others, and this behaviour, being learnt, is fragile and can disappear rather easily under social conditions that no longer teach it effectively (pp.191–193).

However, many contemporary scholars now cite a growing body of empirical evidence that parental behaviours are not simply the consequence of biology and human nature, but rather are informed by cultural, historical and social values, circumstances and processes. In fact, as gender ideologies shifted in the last half of the 20th century, so too did researchers' exploration of variations in men's and women's behaviour generally, and fathering and mothering specifically (Rohner and Veneziano, 2001; Sanchez and Thomson, 1997). Moreover, contemporary perspectives on fatherhood and motherhood are in large part derived from research that concurrently studied fathers and mothers, rather than earlier research that focused almost exclusively on mothers.

Similarities and differences in fathers' and mothers' interactions with offspring

Much of the research into parent-child relations has been informed by the belief that mothers influence children's physical, emotional, psychological and social well-being through expressive and affective behaviours, including warmth and nurturance (Bowlby, 1969; Hojat, 1999; Mahler and Furer, 1968; Phares, 1992; Stern, 1995), whereas fathers have often been viewed as influencing children's development through the instrumental roles of provider and protector, and as role models for social, cognitive, psychological and gender-identity development (Bronstein, 1988; Gilmore, 1990; Lamb and Oppenheim, 1989; Mackey, 1996; Parsons and Bales, 1955; Radin, 1981b). However, contemporary research suggests that maternal behaviour is not situated exclusively in the expressive sphere any more than paternal behaviour is situated exclusively in the instrumental one. Indeed, multivariate research in the 1990s demonstrated the importance of paternal expressive and affective behaviours despite the fact that mothers are often characterized as 'superior caregivers', whereas fathers are viewed as 'less capable of, and/or less interested in, nurturant parenting' (*Parents' Interactions with Offspring*, Hosley and Montemayor, 1997, p.175). As discussed below, fathers' and mothers' behaviours are in fact multidimensional and multifaceted, and these behaviours often vary as a result of contextual variables including youths' age and gender.

Youths' age and gender

According to Collins and Russell (1991), research in Western societies shows that fathers and mothers interact differently with their middle childhood (i.e., preteens) to adolescent children than with younger children. For example, fathers generally interact with their adolescents through focusing on instrumental goals (e.g., school and athletic achievement, future plans) and objective issues such as political discussions. Mothers' interactions with adolescents, on the other hand, tend to be marked more by discussions of personal issues. More specifically, in their review of the literature on US families, Collins and Russell (1991) reported that 15- to 16-year-old US adolescents spent twice as much time alone with their mothers as with their fathers. Collins and Russell also reported that 14- to 18-year-olds, more than 12- to 13-year-olds, spent more time alone with their mothers than with their fathers. As for middle childhood, Collins and Russell (1991) found that mothers tend to be more involved in caregiving, whereas fathers are more involved in play activities.

Questions 1–4

*Read the following passage and select **TWO** correct answers from the FIVE options (**A–E**).*

1   Until the late 20th century, academic views of child development considered that

   A   men were naturally predisposed to childcare.

   B   the father was not an important figure.

   C   fathers failed to provide for their children.

   D   the mother's role was central to child rearing.

   E   men should spend more time with their children.

2   Margaret Mead believed that

   A   women did not want to change society.

   B   fathering could not be learnt.

   C   mothers were genetically programmed to bond with their babies.

   D   the mother-child relationship was difficult to change.

   E   fathers naturally wanted to look after their children.

3   Modern research has discovered that

   A   parenting is not an instinct.

   B   the role of parents varies with external factors.

   C   men and women have fixed parental roles.

   D   motherhood had not been thoroughly researched.

   E   fatherhood had been carefully researched in the past.

4   According to traditional research,

   A   fathers had no effect on their children's intellectual growth.

   B   fathers were not loving by nature.

   C   mothers were responsible for a child's emotional development.

   D   the development of the child's social identity depended on the father.

   E   mothers were not naturally caring.

Questions 5–8

*Complete the sentences in Questions 5–8 with words taken from the passage. Write **NO MORE THAN ONE WORD**.*

5 Early research into .... largely ignored the importance of the role of fatherhood.

6 Modern research has found that emotional behaviour is not restricted to the .... role.

7 The age and gender of the children affects their .... with their parents.

8 When children are in their teens they talk to their mothers more about .... concerns.

Questions 9–13

*Match each sentence beginning (**9–13**) with the correct ending (**A–H**) from the list below.*

9 Modern research into parental roles differs from early research in that

10 It is now more widely accepted for

11 In 1991, Collins and Russell found that children aged 14 to 18

12 In spite of recent changes in parental roles,

13 Even at the end of the 20th century, research found

A men to be affectionate towards their children.

B fathers still tend to concentrate more on their children's tangible achievements than on their emotional problems.

C spent more time with their fathers than with their mothers.

D only paternal roles have been investigated.

E that young children received more nurturing from their mothers.

F spent more time with their mothers than children aged 12 to 13.

G it takes into account changing attitudes to gender.

H that fathers preferred to spend time with their adolescent children.

A Predicting the vocabulary in a passage

1 Look at the images and answer the following questions.

a What are these images about?
b Write down all the words you associate with the images.
c Classify these words into nouns, verbs, adjectives and adverbs.

Skills

Identifying word forms

Developing your vocabulary is one way of improving your reading comprehension. You can read faster and with more understanding if you know how words are constructed, particularly if you can identify prefixes and suffixes.

Prefixes are added at the beginning of words and change their meaning. For example: *act* = to do something, but re + *act* → **re**act = act in response to something else.

B

Suffixes are added at the end of words and change their form. For example: *act* = verb, but act + **ion** → *action* = a noun.

> Hey, have you heard what's trending on Twitter?

> No. What's going on?

> Go to #thelatenews and find out.

2 Combine the words below with prefixes and suffixes to form new words. Some can be combined with more than one prefix or suffix. Others can be combined with a prefix and a suffix.

Example: inter + nation + al.

A create   **B** nation   **C** communicate   **D** act   **E** organize
F entertain   **G** relate   **H** friend   **I** media   **J** social

Prefixes: inter- re- multi- anti- dis-

Suffixes: -al -ive -tivity -ion/-tion/-ation -ment -ship

3 Complete the following text with the correct form of the words in Exercise 2. For some questions there may be two possible words with a similar meaning.

The vast majority of people use social networking sites to
1 _____ with friends and **2** _____ , in other
words people with whom they already have a **3** _____ . It is
not at all uncommon to find school children chatting online in the evening
to classmates they have spent all day with. In some ways, it could be said
that online chats have replaced the personal contact or face-to-face
4 _____ that children used to enjoy after school. In addition to
chat, young people share music and **5** _____ with their friends
through **6** _____ links on their social websites.

Exam skills

Identifying information questions

In questions that require you to decide if a statement is true or false according to information in the passage, it is useful to recognize prefixes that express negatives and to be aware of words with opposite meanings (antonyms).

4 Use your knowledge of prefixes and antonyms to change the following words from positive to negative.

a likely **b** agree **c** accessible **d** understand **e** logical **f** normal **g** justified **h** regulate

5 Look up the following verbs in the dictionary and find their opposites. There may be more than one possible answer.

a allow **b** accept **c** include **d** provide **e** expand **f** contact (v) **g** show **h** maintain

6 Choose the sentence (A–C) that has the same meaning as the statement in questions 1–5.

1 The uses people make of social networking websites are unlikely to increase in the future.
  A In the future, people will probably use social networks on the Internet in a wider variety of ways.
  B It is probable that the different ways people use online social networks will not increase any further.
  C A future increase in the ways people use online social networking is very possible.

2 About 60% of people who use online networking sites are concerned that their personal details may be accessible to people they do not know.
  A Most online social network users do not worry that strangers might be able to see details of their private lives.
  B Only a minority of users of social networking sites are anxious about sharing personal information with people they have not met.
  C Over half the people who use social networking sites are worried that strangers might have access to details of their personal lives.

3 Since 2011 there has been an increase in the number of people who mistrust what they read on social networking websites.
  A More people trust the information they see on social networking sites than in 2011.
  B Fewer users are suspicious of the details they find on social networks than in 2011.
  C A smaller number of social network users trust the information they see online than in 2011.

4 The majority of online social network users control the privacy settings on their profiles to prevent strangers from seeing their details.
  A Older users of online social networking sites are more likely to share personal details with strangers.
  B Most users of social networking sites do not allow people they do not know to access their personal information.
  C Not many people who use online networking sites know how to control who sees their private information.

5 More online users of social networking sites over the age of 45 allow strangers to see their photos than other groups.
  A People over the age of 45 only give access to their photos to people they do not know.
  B Adults in the over-45 age group are more likely to show their photos online to people they have not met in person.
  C Younger users of social networking sites are more likely than older age groups to share their pictures with strangers.

Exam skills

Labelling a diagram

In this type of question you will be asked to complete the labels on a graph or diagram with information from a reading passage. Scan the text for numbers and comparisons to find key information.

7 Read the passage and complete the graph. Write NO MORE THAN THREE WORDS OR A NUMBER from the passage.

> A recent survey into the use of social networking websites has found that a large majority (80%) of adult members use the sites to chat online to friends or family they see a lot. A slightly lower percentage (76%) talk to members of the family they rarely see. Looking for old friends is only 1% less popular than looking at other people's pages (45%). The same percentage of users of social networking sites (25%) 'like' products and services and invite people to social events, while 23% of users go online to find out about events in the neighbourhood. 21% of online users log on to social networking sites to find out about bands and to read the sporting news. A slightly smaller percentage (17%) use social networks to share video clips. It is surprising that only 15% of social network users take advantage of the medium to extend their business or professional networks, and even fewer (10%) use social networks to advertise or promote their business. Finally, it is interesting to note that, contrary to popular belief, fewer than 4% of adults use social networking sites for dating.

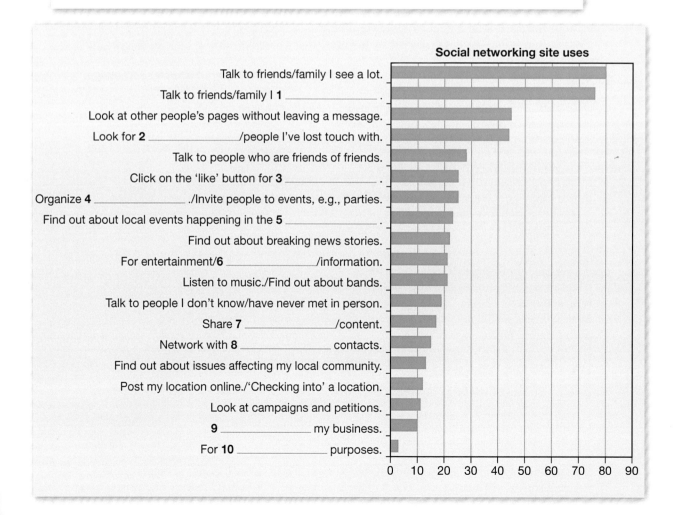

Exam skills

Summary questions

In this type of question you are asked to complete a summary of part of a passage, usually with only one word, using words from a list of options. As the information in the passage will not necessarily be in the same order as the summary, you may need to scan the section several times for the correct information. Remember the words in the list may not be the same as in the passage. You will need to look for words which have a similar meaning.

8 Read the following passage and complete the summary with words from the list in the box.

Could Facebook help predict obesity hotspots? Areas where people who 'like' TV more than sport are less healthy

Emma Innes

– People with television-related Facebook 'interests' are more likely to be obese.

– Those related to a healthy lifestyle are less likely to have weight issues.

– People's online 'interests' could help predict and map obesity rates by area.

Facebook could be a key tool in mapping which geographical areas have the most overweight and obese people. American researchers have found that the higher the percentage of people in a city or town with Facebook 'interests' suggesting a healthy lifestyle, the lower that area's obesity rate. At the same time, areas with a large percentage of Facebook users with television-related 'interests' tend to have higher rates of obesity.

Researchers at Boston Children's Hospital, in the US, drew these conclusions after comparing Facebook user data with data from national and New York City-focused health surveys. They looked at what Facebook users posted to their timeline, 'liked' and shared with others. They then compared the percentage of users interested in healthy activities or television with details of Body Mass Index in the same area. The comparison revealed close geographic relationships between Facebook 'interests' and obesity rates.

For instance, the obesity rate was 12 per cent lower in the location in the United States where the highest percentage of Facebook users expressed activity-related 'interests', compared with that in the location with the lowest percentage.

Similarly, the obesity rate in the location with the highest percentage of users with television-related interests nationally was 3.9 per cent higher than the location with the lowest percentage.

The same correlation was reflected in the New York City neighbourhood data as well, showing that the approach can scale from national to local-level data.

The obesity rate on Coney Island, which had the highest percentage of activity-related 'interests' in the city, was 7.2 per cent lower than Southwest Queens, the neighbourhood with the lowest percentage. At the same time, the obesity rate in Northeast Bronx, the neighbourhood with the highest percentage of television-related 'interests', was 27.5 per cent higher than that in the neighbourhood with the lowest percentage – Greenpoint.

They now believe that people's online 'interests' could help public health researchers predict, track and map obesity rates by area. The amount of data available from social networks like Facebook makes it possible to efficiently carry out research with cohorts of a size that was previously impossible. Dr John Brownstein, from Boston Children's Hospital, explained: 'Online social networks like Facebook represent a new high-value, low-cost data stream for looking at health at a population level. 'The tight correlation between Facebook users' "interests" and obesity data suggest that this kind of social network analysis could help generate real-time estimates of obesity levels in an area, help target public health campaigns that would promote healthy behaviour change, and assess the success of those campaigns.'

Summary

Recent research in a number of cities and neighbourhoods in the US has discovered a significant relationship between official figures for the number of people who are

1 _____ and the type of 2 _____ interests registered by users of Facebook in that area. In 3 _____ where Facebook users expressed a preference for 4 _____ activities, lower levels of obesity were recorded than cities where users had more 5 _____ interests like watching television. This close correlation between official public health data and information collected from Facebook promises to facilitate research into 6 _____ health patterns, and will, in turn, assist local 7 _____ in targeting their public health programmes more 8 _____ .

strategically ■ authorities ■ sporting ■ overweight ■ regional ■ leisure ■ districts ■ passive

Reading Passage 7

You should spend 20 minutes on questions 1–13, which are based on Reading Passage 7.

Their social life online: a parents' guide

Rachel Carlyle

Worried parents take heart – a growing body of research shows that teens who use social media are not reclusive geeks: they actually have a wider circle of real-life friends, a better sense of identity and belonging and are developing the essential technical skills they need to be citizens of a digital age.

'Social networking has become an embedded part of modern childhood,' says e-safety pioneer Stephen Carrick-Davies, who advises parents and schools on technology.

'Children do not consume media – dipping in and out to buy airline tickets or check emails as adults do – they inhabit it. That's neither good nor bad – it's what you do with it that counts.'

What teenagers mainly do with it is socialize with friends they already know. 'It's the modern equivalent of hanging around at the bus stop to share the in-jokes and catch up on the gossip: a kind of virtual bus stop,' says Tim Mungeam, a parenting consultant who runs social networking seminars for teens and their parents.

And it performs a similar function: helping teenagers develop a sense of identity away from their parents and learning to get on with their peers. Professor Kevin Durkin, a psychologist at Strathclyde University, says: 'Adolescence is a time when you are asking, who am I? Who do I want to become? Social networking can help you develop that self-identity: you can post notices about your favourite music or sports, discover what you enjoy, and you are constantly reminded that other people have different ways of looking at things and have different tastes. Research actually shows that keen social networkers are not as self-absorbed as others who don't.'

He says that embracing social media can also help shy teens blossom: 'They tend to find computer-mediated communication more comfortable than face-to-face, and there may be benefits from practising social skills in a less-threatening environment.'

Professor Andy Phippen, of Plymouth University, who is researching the use of social networking sites by teenagers, feels that these sites can also boost the confidence of children traditionally on the edge of friendship groups. 'Unlike in our day, when there were the Alpha* kids and those very much on the periphery of friendship groups, social networking can bring in the ones on the periphery so there's not so much difference between them,' he says.

It can be a life-saver for the quiet, geeky child who has a specialized interest because it can allow them to connect with others with similar interests. 'If you are one of only three kids in your school in Cornwall who is into Emo* culture, traditionally you would have felt quite isolated. But if you discover a social networking group of like-minded teenagers, there's suddenly a necessary critical mass and you can still be popular, just in a different context,' Professor Phippen adds.

Experts always used to advise monitoring your children's social networking activities, but there is a growing consensus that once they reach 13 or 14, and parents are happy they know the ground rules (stay civil, be kind, don't give out personal details to those you don't know in real life) they should trust them to get on with it.

It's the teenagers who are able to find new interests online, join networks of likeminded individuals – and then create their own content – who are really harnessing the potential of social networks, says Pamela Whitby, the digital education expert and author of *Is Your Child Safe Online?*

'Social networking is becoming a creative force: teenagers are making videos, joining YouTube groups, podcasting and blogging about the things that interest them. Sites like Pinterest, which is like a digital look-book, and Instagram, a photosharing network, are transforming creativity, and I think niche networks are going to become more and more common.

'I recently went into a school and thought I would be telling all these teenagers about how to use Instagram – but many were already using it. The keen photographers were networking with each other, learning skills, swapping images and deepening their own interest. This all adds to their employability and will undoubtedly benefit them in the workplace.

'Every single business is using social media to sell and to increase brand-awareness – and you need to understand how it works and how it can create customers. For example, if you develop a product and you have 700 friends on Facebook and 300 on other networks, they are all potential customers for that product. If you link all those networks together there's your customer base right there.'

Teenagers who use social networking as a creative force will reap the benefits in the world of work, agrees Mungeam. 'One of the fantastic aspects of Facebook and YouTube is the opportunity for collaborating with others to create content, then sharing it with others. Collaboration is a real 21st-century skill, and an essential part of being employable in a digital age.

'Social networking helps them find out what they are passionate about. They can be in touch with people all over the world sharing ideas and gradually they can build their online reputation: signing up to campaigns or joining groups to make their voice heard.

'Social networks amplify one person's voice, and no one appreciates this more than a teenager.'

Teenagers who use social networks will reap the benefits in the world of work.

* **Alpha kids** – most dominant children in a group
* **Emo** – a style of music/a community of emotionally sensitive people

---

Questions 1–5

*Do the following statements agree with the information in the text? Write **TRUE**, **FALSE** or **NOT GIVEN**.*

1   Social media discourages adolescents from developing real friends.

2   Young people use the Internet to book tickets for concerts.

3   The majority of teenagers use online networking sites to meet new people.

4   Socializing online helps teenagers to collaborate with people of their own age.

5   Teenagers who socialize online tend to be more introverted than others.

Questions 6–7

*Label the diagram with words taken from the passage. Write **NO MORE THAN ONE WORD**.*

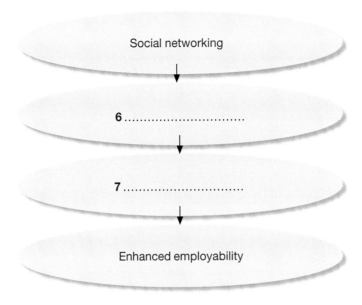

Skills that improve employability

Social networking

6 ....

7 ....

Enhanced employability

Questions 8–13

*Complete the summary with letters (**A–H**) from the list in the box.*

NB *There are two extra words on the list.*

Early research into **8** .... and social media suggested that teenagers who socialized online might be afraid of mixing with their **9** .... in real life. However, recent research has shown that adolescents who 'meet up' with their friends on social networking sites are actually less **10** ...., have a stronger sense of their own **11** .... and have more real friends than those who do not. Furthermore, online networking sites can offer less- **12** .... adolescents a safe platform from which to interact with their social circle, potentially reducing the distance between more assertive, popular group members and **13** .... individuals, who traditionally hover on the edges of their social group.

A quieter

B adolescence

C identity

D intelligence

E peers

F isolated

G confident

H parents

Caring
for the elderly

READING SKILLS
Analysing information
Recognizing the structure of an argument
Identifying the writer's views

EXAM PRACTICE
Completing notes
Matching features
Yes/No/Not Given

Predicting the writer's views

1 Look at these newspaper headlines and answer the questions.

> **A**   **Neglect in care homes for elderly**

> **B**   There's no place like home for the elderly

> **C**   GRANNY FIGHTS FOR RIGHT TO WORK

> **D**   **Pensions at seventy: a solution for the future**

   a   What issues are raised in each of these headlines?
   b   Do you think these problems are the same in every country? Why?
   c   Which headlines suggest a positive, negative or neutral viewpoint? How do
       you know?

Skills

Identifying the writer's views

The writer's attitude towards the topic of the text can be expressed in several
ways, for example, through the use of:

   a   vocabulary that has positive or negative connotations or associated meanings
       (*kind, strong, motherly, deceitful, undecided, lazy*).
   b   modal verbs that suggest doubt (*might/may/could*).
   c   vocabulary that suggests degrees of probability (*possibly, likely*).
   d   structuring sentences to emphasize or focus on a particular point ('*Because he
       was over 60*, he found it difficult to find a new job.').

2 Read the following passage and underline examples of each of these techniques.

> Over the last century, perceptions of the elderly have changed for a number
> of reasons. Improved health, longer life expectancy and greater potential for
> a productive contribution to society are amongst these. There can be little
> doubt that in recent centuries, better nourishment, combined with impressive
> advances in both preventative and curative medicine, has led to increased
> longevity. Thus, it is reasonable to assume that this extended lifespan might
> possibly be accompanied by a longer working life and later retirement.

3 Which sentences in the passage state facts and which sentences express the writer's opinion?

4 Select the word in each group that does not have positive connotations.
  a healthy   energetic   dynamic   exhausted   experienced
  b powerful   capable   obstructive   creative   imaginative
  c weary   intelligent   helpful   wise   sensible
  d family   friends   home   care   ignorance
  e improve   deteriorate   strong   tolerant   optimistic

5 Read the following sentences (a–e) and underline the words that indicate degrees of certainty.
  a Continuing to work into later life has definite health benefits.
  b People who continue to work into their later years may enjoy better health than people who retire early.
  c There is a slight possibility that early retirement could lead to a deterioration in health.
  d Working longer almost certainly keeps people healthy.
  e There can be no question that later retirement results in better health.

6 Number the sentences (a–e) in Exercise 5 in order of the degree of certainty (1 = very certain, 5 = very uncertain).

Exam skills

Yes/No/Not Given questions

In questions that require you to decide whether a statement agrees or disagrees with the writer's opinion, first check whether the writer explicitly makes a claim or not, then look carefully for words or phrases that indicate a positive or negative view.

Skills

7 Read the following passage and check which topics (a–f) are mentioned in the text. Write a tick (✓) on the line if they are mentioned and a cross (✗) if they are not.

  a residential options for the elderly _____

  b the opinions of the elderly about their housing options _____

  c the facilities available in extra care housing _____

  d the cost of accommodation in retirement communities _____

  e the facilities available in care homes _____

  f the amount of control older people have over their lives _____

> A Housing with care, such as extra care housing (ECH) or continuing care retirement communities, has been promoted as a purpose-built, community-based alternative to moving into residential care for older people (e.g., Department of Health, 2005). It aims to meet the housing, care and support needs of older people, while helping them to maintain
> 5 independence in private accommodation (Department of Health, 2008), and is seen as a positive option for older people in current social care policy (Department of Health, 2010). Key features of ECH are that it is primarily for older people; accommodation is self-contained; care is delivered flexibly by staff often based on site; staff are available 24 hours a day; domestic care is available; meals are usually available; and it offers
> 10 security of tenure (Laing and Buisson, 2010). The expectation is that ECH will afford older

people a greater sense of control over their lives than more institutional settings, such as care homes, whilst avoiding the pitfalls of 'staying put', such as disjointed care, social isolation and inappropriate housing.

B There have been several studies in which older people living in ECH have been asked
15 about their experiences and have reported high levels of satisfaction (see Croucher, Hicks and Jackson, 2006). Feeling that they have retained more control over their lives than they would have in residential care is frequently mentioned as being valued. However, the evidence has largely come from evaluations of new and innovative housing with care schemes, which market themselves as promoting independence and providing positive
20 alternatives to institutional models of care (Croucher, Hicks and Jackson, 2006). In fact, a recent study of the expectations and experiences of older people moving into residential care (Darton, 2011) suggests that the expectation that residential care is associated with a total loss of control and independence can be overly pessimistic. Most of the 69 residents, interviewed after settling into a care home, told researchers they had more control over
25 their lives than they had expected before moving in and the percentage rating their quality of life as good or very good rose by 12 per cent (Darton, 2011). Furthermore, Boyle (2004) found that older people in residential care experienced the most control and people receiving domiciliary care the least, when she conducted semi-structured interviews with older people living in care homes (residential and nursing) or in the community.

30 **C** Surprisingly, studies such as Boyle's (2004) are difficult to find in the UK literature. There has been seemingly little research directly comparing older people's sense of control in different care settings, despite the policy agenda. Most research has tended to look more broadly at older people's experiences in a single setting: care homes (Bowers et al, 2009; Darton, 2011; Kane et al, 2004; Raynes, 1998; Taylor et al, 2009; Train et al, 2005); ECH (Bäumker
35 et al, 2012; Callaghan, Netten and Darton, 2009; see also Croucher, Hicks and Jackson, 2006 for a review); or home care (Aronson, 2002; Barrett, Hale and Gauld, 2012; EHRC, 2011; Raynes et al, 2001). Where comparisons have been made, they have tended to focus on broader quality of life issues or physical and cognitive functioning, and have focused on comparing two main care options, such as extra care to domiciliary care (Bernard et al,
40 2007; Gardner, Browning and Kendig, 2005; Kingston et al, 2001; Kneale, 2011), extra care to residential care (Darton et al, 2011a) or domiciliary care to residential care (Boyle, 2004).

8 Scan the passage again and underline the words or phrases that express possibility, doubt or potential.

9 Scan the passage again and underline the words that have positive connotations.

10 Read paragraph A of the passage and decide whether the following statements agree with the views expressed in the text. Write *YES*, *NO* or *NOT GIVEN* next to statements a–d.

   a The Department of Health supports the development of extra care housing. _____

   b Extra care housing is becoming increasingly popular amongst the elderly. _____

   c Policy makers believe that supported housing schemes will prevent the elderly from controlling their lives. _____

   d Not receiving appropriate medical attention is one of the disadvantages of staying at home in later years. _____

Exam skills

Matching features

In one type of question you are asked to match a series of statements to a list of options which represent the characteristics of a specific group; for example, a field of science, a school of art or philosophy. The instructions will tell you if you can use the options more than once. The questions are in the same order as the information in the text.

Skills

11 Match the following statements (1–3) with the names of the researchers (A–C).

1 Residents in extra care housing schemes believed they were more in control of their lives than they would have been in care homes.

2 Residents in care homes felt they controlled more aspects of their lives than they had previously anticipated.

3 In comparison with people who live in residential homes, people who were cared for in their own homes felt they had less control over their lives.

List of researchers
A Darton
B Croucher, Hicks and Jackson
C Boyle

Skills

Recognizing the structure of an argument

You can follow the logical argument in a text by taking note of the organizational words and phrases that indicate the relationship between the different ideas. These linking terms will show whether the author intends to:

a supply additional information.
b give an example or an illustration of an idea.
c contrast one idea with another.
d compare ideas.
e describe the consequences of events.
f summarize several ideas.
g state a condition.

12 Match the linking words (1–10) with their organizational function (a–g). Some functions can be matched with more than one word.

1 moreover	_____	6 thus	_____
2 however	_____	7 such as	_____
3 but	_____	8 furthermore	_____
4 whatever	_____	9 in brief	_____
5 as ... as	_____	10 leading to	_____

Exam skills

Completing notes

In this type of question you may be asked to complete notes with a certain number of words taken from the reading passage. The instructions will tell you exactly how many words to use. If you use more, you will lose points.

13 Read the passage and complete the notes. Write NO MORE THAN TWO WORDS from the passage.

Number working beyond State Pension Age doubles over past two decades

The number of older workers, defined here as those working beyond State Pension Age (SPA), has almost doubled from 753 thousand in 1993 to 1.4 million in 2011. Over the period, the number remained relatively flat between 1993 and 2000 but quickly rose to a peak of 1.45 million in 2010.

Over the period, with an ageing population and with the post-World War II 'baby boom' generation reaching SPA, the population of older people has increased. Likewise, looking at the percentage of the older population in employment this too has increased from 7.6 per cent in 1993 to 12 per cent in 2011. This shows that the number of workers above SPA has risen at a faster rate than the population.

There may be many factors influencing the decision for more people to work past SPA, such as the improved health and well-being of this group, financial pressures, people living longer and wanting to remain active in society, and others.

Now focusing on the final quarter of 2011, workers over SPA were more likely to be self-employed than their younger counterparts (those aged between 16 up to SPA). Around 32 per cent of workers above SPA were self-employed compared to just 13 per cent of those below SPA.

Also, workers over SPA were twice as likely to be working part-time (66 per cent) than full-time (34 per cent). For those under SPA, three-quarters (75 per cent) worked full-time and the remaining 25 per cent worked part-time.

This shows that when working over the State Pension Age, those remaining in the labour market work fewer hours, possibly helped by the financial support of their state pension and other pension arrangements, which allows them to fit their work around other engagements.

Workers over State Pension Age (SPA)

Statistics: 1993: 753 000   2010: 1.45m   2011: 1.4m

Reason for increase:

- after WWII **1** _____ rose rapidly
- post-war **2** _____ is staying in **3** _____ longer

Reasons for continuing to work:

- **4** _____ concerns, better health, more **5** _____ lifestyle

Older worker profile:

- 32 % **6** _____
- 66% **7** _____

Reasons for work pattern:

- income from **8** _____ , more flexibility

Reading Passage 8

You should spend 20 minutes on questions 1–14, which are based on Reading Passage 8.

How can retirement affect health?

This analysis raises an important question: is the decreased labour force participation rate partly responsible for the improvements in general health? This question is important. If a longer working life induces health deterioration, then a policy of trying to encourage people to work longer will be much less attractive. Furthermore, since healthcare is mostly publicly funded in the UK, a decline in health as a result of policies that induce longer working lives may lead to increases in health spending. At the same time, of course, such policies would also produce more suffering among the elderly, who would pay for their labour force participation with poorer health.

On the other hand, it is also possible that retirement may be to the detriment of health, so policies to induce longer working lives could, in fact, produce even better improvements in life expectancy and healthy life expectancy. In fact, Milligan and Wise (2012) find little relationship between mortality and employment rates at the country level. For any given mortality rate, the employment rate among older men varies significantly across countries, and changes in mortality within countries are weak predictors of changes in employment rates of older men. However, mortality is a rather crude measure of health. Secondly, it is not necessarily the case that the apparently non-existent relationship between employment and health holds up in microlevel analyses. Indeed, the evidence clearly suggests deteriorations in health-induced retirement at the individual level in the British context (Disney et al, 2006).

Theoretically, the impact of retirement on health is far from certain. According to the human capital model of Grossman (2000), good health is crucial for allowing individuals to maximize their utility. Health has an impact on utility directly through its effect on people's life satisfaction and happiness while also reducing work-related illness which, in turn, allows people to raise their total earnings. The former mechanism may lead people to invest more in their health after retirement – since they have more time to enjoy their leisure activities – whereas the latter mechanism may lead them to invest less, since they no longer have a job with which to increase their earnings. Whether incentives to invest in health increase or decrease after retirement depends on whether the marginal benefit of better health is higher or lower compared with before retirement, and there is no straightforward correct answer regarding which scenario is correct (Dave et al, 2006). Additionally, it is important to note that health investments may change prior to retirement, since individuals engage in retirement planning, the effects of which may kick in once they have retired. Also it should be noted that investment in health may not be primarily monetary investments. They can include making changes to diet, developing a daily exercise routine, and so on.

Other mechanisms by which retirement can affect health appear equally ambiguous. The social capital literature*, for example, indicates beneficial effects of trust and social interactions on health (for example, see Petrou and Kupek, 2008; d'Hombres et al, 2010, Ronconi et al, 2012). It is plausible that retirement can reduce social networks if these mostly stemmed from a person's job. However, the retired also have more leisure time, which can be used to establish new social contacts outside work. Additionally, retired people have more time to devote to voluntary work, which is also a base from which new contacts can be established.

Equally, while stress is clearly detrimental to health, the impact of retirement on stress is also not clear-cut. Retirement is an important life event that can be very stressful, but it can also decrease work-related pressure. The same applies for physical exercise. Some people get most of their exercise from work, whereas retirement may allow others to exercise more on a voluntary basis. Indeed, the impact of retirement on exercise appears to vary depending on the type of people and the type of job from which they exit (Chung et al, 2009; Kuvaja-Köllner et al, 2012).

Another mechanism by which retirement affects health is through what is termed the 'income effect'. When people retire, they are likely to see a drop in their income. This, in turn, might affect their health negatively.

Furthermore, it is important to note that the health impact of retirement is not necessarily linear: immediate and short-term effects may differ significantly from medium- and long-term impacts. The mechanisms linking retirement to health can involve very long delays. It is clearly plausible that the longer-term health effects of retirement can differ significantly from the short-term impact. For example, the reduction in stress may have a beneficial short-term impact but the reduced social contact may have a detrimental longer-term impact.

* **social capital** – a network of beneficial social connections

Questions 1–5

*Do the following statements match the views of the writer? Write **YES**, **NO** or **NOT GIVEN**.*

1   If continuing to work into later years harms people's health, the cost of public healthcare will increase.

2   The death rate is not a very precise way of assessing health levels.

3   There is a very clear relationship between retirement and health.

4   Retired people prefer voluntary work to paid employment.

5   People generally exercise more when they retire.

Questions 6–9

Match the research themes with the names of the researchers (A–D).

6 the correlation between age at death and continued employment

7 the relationship between good health and income

8 the effect of socializing on health

9 retirement and fitness

Researchers

A Chung et al

B Milligan and Wise

C Grossman

D Ronconi et al

Questions 10–14

*Read the passage and complete the notes with words from the passage. Write **NO MORE THAN ONE WORD**.*

Retirement

Stress:

- reduced because of less **10** .... at work

- increased because process of retirement is **11** ....

Exercise in retirement:

- decreases when employment was based on **12** .... activity

- increases with more time for **13** .... keep-fit sessions

Effects:

- short-term: positive – more time to relax

- long-term: negative – less **14** .... interaction

Rising sea levels
and climate change

UNIT AIMS

READING SKILLS
Classifying information
Recognizing trends
Skimming for key data

EXAM PRACTICE
Labelling a map
Completing a table
Short answer questions

Identifying the topic

1 Look at these images and answer the questions.
  a How are these images connected?
  b Could you organize these pictures in a different order? Explain how you would decide.
  c Do you think global warming is the result of human activity? Give reasons for your opinion.

Skills

Classifying information

Before you read a text you can ask yourself a few questions:

1 Does the title give me a clear idea of the content?
  • The title of a text about factual events may give you important clues about the topic, focus, date and location of the information.
2 Do I know anything about this topic?
  • If you know something about the topic, think of the key vocabulary you might expect to find in the text. Try to remember alternative words (synonyms) associated with these key words.
3 What kind of information can I expect to find in the passage?
  • The title might refer to some or several of the following: dates, percentages, figures, currency, geographical locations, volumes, ratios and measurements.
4 Can I predict the structure of the text from the title?
  • The time frame and the tense of the verb in the title will indicate whether the text will describe past events or the current situation or predict future developments.

2 Read the following titles of articles about rising sea levels and answer questions 1–4 above.
  a Sea level change – 100 years of annual tide-gauge records
  b Rate of acceleration of global mean sea-level rise since 2000
  c US east coast cities affected by two-metre rise in ocean levels
  d Nineteenth and twentieth century rises in sea level

3 Scan the passage below and complete the table with the type of information found in the text.

Dates/Periods of time	Measurements	Geographical locations

Sea level rising

Global average sea level has increased over 8 inches since 1880, and global warming has caused the great majority, if not all, of that rise. Warming has acted in two main ways: by heating up and thus expanding the global ocean; and by attacking glaciers and polar ice sheets, pouring meltwater and icebergs into the sea. The planet has heated by more than one degree Fahrenheit over the last century, rising faster as we have burnt coal, oil and gas faster, and so sent ever more heat-trapping gases into the air. Scientists overwhelmingly agree that these building gases are responsible for most of the warming observed thus far.

Warming and sea-level rise are both accelerating, as is the rate of decay of ice sheets on Greenland and Antarctica. Loss of ice from these sources has the potential to raise sea level by many tens of feet over centuries. In the warm period before the last Ice Age – when the planet was as warm as we expect it to become by 2100 or sooner, at least without deep and immediate cuts to pollution – global sea level very likely reached over 20 feet higher than it is today, an eventual sea level we could be committing to within decades if not already. That rise would be enough to drown many major coastal metropolises.

This century, scientists expect about 20 to 80 more inches of global sea-level rise, depending significantly on how much more heat-trapping pollution humankind puts into the sky. The amount also depends on just how strongly pollution translates into warming, and just how strongly warming translates into sea rise.

4 Complete the following sentences with the correct tense of the verbs in brackets.

a Over the last 130 years the sea level _____ (rise) nearly 10 inches.

b Even now the volume of the ocean _____ (expand) as the planet gets warmer and polar ice melts.

c Experts calculate that over the next century human activity _____ (cause) sea levels to match those of the Ice Age.

Skills

Recognizing trends in charts, diagrams, tables and maps

Texts that give factual information often include statistics and figures that can also be represented in charts, diagrams, tables and maps. In the text, the writer will usually:

a describe the data or information.
b compare figures over a period of time, or at different points in time.
c highlight the most significant aspects of the data; for example, exceptionally high and low figures, percentages and ratios in a chart, unusual data patterns, exceptions to the norm and trends.
d explain the possible causes of and reasons for the figures and changes in the chart.

Exam skills

Labelling a map

In some questions you will be asked to complete labels on a map using words or numbers from the reading passage. You can write numbers in figures or words, but remember that in the reading test spelling counts. If you write the numbers in words, you must take care to spell them correctly.

5 Read the following passage and complete the map with the predicted rise in sea level that will completely submerge each city. Write a NUMBER from the text.

Rising sea levels threaten coastal cities

Since 1880, sea levels have risen an average of 8 inches globally. Calculations vary, but there is common consensus that, as a result of global warming, oceans will heat up and expand at an increasing pace and sea levels will consequently rise more rapidly. Some scientists calculate that the sea will rise between 6 and 15 inches by 2050 and between 12 and 48 inches by 2100. Experts predict that if this trend continues, many coastal settlements will be susceptible to flooding within the next century, and that some will be in danger of disappearing altogether.

Unusually high tides and storm surges in recent years, have already caused serious flooding in cities worldwide, including New York, New Orleans and Venice. Although, this in itself does not pose an immediate threat to their survival, there is evidence that rising sea levels could lead to the inundation of major cities by the end of the 21st century.

If scientific calculations are accurate, Venice would be completely submerged if sea levels rose by 42 inches. The Hague in Holland, another low-lying European city, would also be affected by rising sea levels. Like Venice, it is only 39 inches above today's sea level, and would be totally submerged if sea levels rose by 45 inches. On the other hand, central New York, at an elevation of 79 inches above sea level, would not be submerged until the level of the ocean rose by 80 inches, while the greater part of San Francisco would disappear under the sea with a rise in sea level of only 42 inches.

Rise in sea levels (in inches) needed to submerge major cities

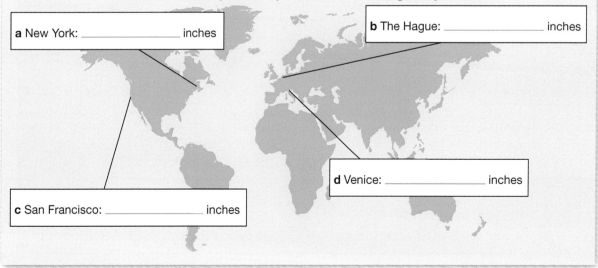

a New York: _____ inches

b The Hague: _____ inches

c San Francisco: _____ inches

d Venice: _____ inches

6 Scan the text again and identify the organizational words and phrases that express relationships of:

    a cause   **b** effect   **c** comparison

Skills

Skimming for key data

Skimming is an effective technique for identifying the overall message and structure of a reading passage (see Unit 1). Key words from the topic sentence are repeated and extended throughout the passage, indicating points in the text where sub-topics and themes are developed. Words and phrases that express opinions and logical arguments outline the structure of the text.

7 Skim the following text for:

a key vocabulary in the topic sentence.
b repetitions of key and associated vocabulary in the text.
c sub-topics or themes.
d words that indicate the logical argument and structure of the text.

Traditional knowledge and past experience

Adaptive capacity and resilience can also be strengthened through the application of traditional knowledge and past experience of environmental changes. In the TAR*, Nurse et al (2001) noted that some traditional island assets, including subsistence and traditional technologies, skills and knowledge, and community structures, and coastal areas containing spiritual, cultural and
5   heritage sites, appeared to be at risk from climate change, and particularly sea-level rise. They argued that some of these values and traditions are compatible with modern conservation and environmental practices.

Since then, several examples of such practices have been described. For instance, Hoffmann (2002) has shown that the implementation of traditional marine social institutions, as exemplified
10   in the Ra'ui in Rarotonga, Cook Islands, is an effective conservation management tool, and is improving coral reef health; while Aswani and Hamilton (2004) show how indigenous* ecological knowledge and customary sea tenure* may be integrated with modern marine and social science to conserve the bumphead parrotfish in Roviana Lagoon, Solomon Islands. Changes in sea tenure, back to more traditional roles, have also occurred in Kiribati (Thomas, 2001).

15   The utility of traditional knowledge and practices can also be expanded to link not only with biodiversity* conservation but also with tourism. For instance, in a coastal village on Vanua Levu, Fiji, the philosophy of *vanua* (which refers to the connection of people with the land through their ancestors and guardian spirits) has served as a guiding principle for the villagers in the management and sustainable use of the rainforest, mangrove forest, coral reefs and village
20   gardens. Sinha and Bushell (2002) have shown that the same traditional concept can be the basis for biodiversity conservation, because the ecological systems upon which the villagers depend for subsistence are the very same resources that support tourism. These examples indicate that local knowledge, management frameworks and skills could be important components of adaptive capacity in those small islands that still have some traditional foundations.

* **TAR** – Third Assessment Report of the Intergovernmental Panel on Climate Change
* **indigenous** – characteristic of a specific region
* **tenure** – possessing or looking after something (usually property)
* **biodiversity** – a variety of plant or animal life

Exam skills

Table completion

One type of question asks you to complete a table which summarizes information from one section of the text. The answers may not be in the same order as the information in the reading passage. You should write the words exactly as they appear in the reading passage. Check the spelling and make sure you do not exceed the number of words you are asked to write.

8 Complete the table with information from the passage on page 73. Write NO MORE THAN THREE WORDS in your answer.

Location	Traditional practice	Beneficial to
Cook Islands	using ancient **a** _____ societies	**b** _____
Solomon Islands and **c** _____	application of local **d** _____ information	bumphead parrot fish
Fiji	consulting with forefathers and **e** _____	forests, coral formations and **f** _____

Exam skills

Short answer questions

In this type of exercise you are required to answer questions about factual details in a reading passage using words from the text. The answers to the questions are in the same order as the information in the text. You must write the number of words indicated in the instructions.

9 Read the passage on page 73 and answer the questions (a–e) with words from the text. Write NO MORE THAN TWO WORDS.

a Where exactly are the cultural and religious places that Nurse et al (2001) consider to be endangered by a rise in sea level? _____

b According to Nurse et al (2001), how do time-honoured community wisdom and current environmental and conservation methods relate? _____

c Which features of managing the sea have been reintroduced in Kiribati? _____

d What role does *vanua* play in the ecological practices of the population of Vanua Levu? _____

e What determines both the islanders' survival and the tourist industry? _____

Reading Passage 9

You should spend 20 minutes on questions 1–13, which are based on Reading Passage 9.

The Antarctic Peninsula is a rugged mountain chain generally more than 2000 metres high, differing from most of Antarctica by having a summer melting season. Summer melt produces many isolated snow-free areas, which are habitats for simple biological communities of primitive plants, microbes and invertebrates*, and breeding grounds for marine mammals and birds. The Antarctic Peninsula has experienced dramatic warming at rates several times the global mean (Vaughan et al, 2003; Trenberth et al, 2007). Since the TAR*, substantial progress has been made in understanding the causes and profound impacts of this warming.

Since records began, 50 years ago, mean annual temperatures on the Antarctic Peninsula have risen rapidly: >2.5°C at Vernadsky (formerly Faraday) Station (Turner et al, 2005). On the west coast, warming has been much slower in summer and spring than in winter or autumn, but has been sufficient to raise the number of positive-degree days by 74% (Vaughan et al, 2003), and the resulting increase in melt has caused dramatic impacts on the Antarctic Peninsula environment, and its ecology.

Around 14 000 km^2 of ice have been lost from 10 floating ice shelves (King, 2003), 87% of glacier termini* have retreated (Cook et al, 2005), and seasonal snow cover has decreased (Fox and Cooper, 1998). The loss of seasonal snow and floating ice do not have a direct impact on global sea level, but acceleration of inland glaciers due to the loss of ice shelves (De Angelis and Skvarca, 2003; Scambos et al, 2004; Rignot et al, 2005) and increased run-off of melt water (Vaughan, 2006) will cause an increase in this contribution. If summer warming continues, these effects will grow.

Marine sediment* cores show that ice shelves probably have not reached a similar minimum for at least 10 000 years (Domack et al, 2005), and certainly not for 1000 years (Pudsey and Evans, 2001; Domack et al, 2003). This suggests that the retreat is not simply due to cyclic variations in local climate, and that recent warming is unique in the past 10 000 years (Turner et al, 2007). The processes leading to warming are unclear, but appear to be correlated with atmospheric circulation (van den Broeke and van Lipzig, 2003) and particularly with changes in the Southern Annular Mode* caused by anthropogenic* influence (Marshall et al, 2004; Marshall et al, 2006). The winter warming on the west coast also appears to be related to persistent retreat of sea ice (Parkinson, 2002) and warming in the Bellingshausen Sea (Meredith and King, 2005). The spring depletion of ozone over Antarctica (the Antarctic Ozone Hole) has also been implicated in driving circulation change (Thompson and Solomon, 2002), but this has been disputed (Marshall et al, 2004). Current general circulation models (GCMs) do not, however, simulate this observed warming over the past 50 years (King, 2003) and we cannot predict with confidence whether rapid warming will continue in the future.

If warming does continue (especially in the summer) there will be significant impacts; retreat of coastal ice and loss of snow cover would result in newly exposed rock and permafrost* – providing new habitats for colonization by expanding and invading flora and fauna. However, the direct impacts of climate change on the flora and fauna are difficult to predict, since these ecosystems are subject to multiple stressors. For example, increased damage by ultraviolet exposure, because of reduced ozone levels and summer desiccation*, may oppose the direct responses to warming (Convey et al, 2002). In addition, there is a growing threat of alien species invasion, as climatic barriers to their establishment are eroded by climate amelioration*, and increasing human activity increases the opportunity for introduction. Such invasions have already occurred on many sub-Antarctic islands, with detrimental consequences for native species (Frenot et al, 2005). Furthermore, slow reproduction rates during rapid climate change may limit the possible relocation of native species.

* **invertebrates** – animals without a backbone
* **TAR** – Third Assessment Report of the Intergovernmental Panel on Climate Change
* **termini** – the end of something
* **sediment** – mineral or organic matter that sits at the bottom of the sea
* **Southern Annular Mode** – climactic patterns occurring in the southern hemisphere
* **anthropogenic** – caused by human activity
* **permafrost** – frozen soil
* **desiccation** – drying
* **amelioration** – improvement

Questions 1–4

*Label the diagram below with information from the text. Write **NO MORE THAN TWO WORDS OR A NUMBER**.*

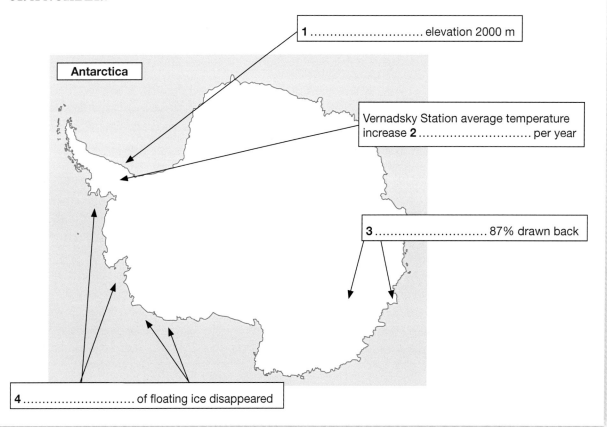

1 .... elevation 2000 m

Antarctica

Vernadsky Station average temperature increase 2 .... per year

3 .... 87% drawn back

4 .... of floating ice disappeared

Questions 5–9

Complete the table with information from the reading passage. Write **NO MORE THAN TWO WORDS OR A NUMBER**.

Year of research publication	Effects on Antarctic	Causes
5	ice shelves smallest in 10 000 years	
6	exceptional levels of warming in last 10 000 years	
2003	higher temperatures	7 ....
2004 and 8	changes in Southern Annular Mode	human activity
2002	west coast 9	reduction in sea ice

Questions 10–13

Answer questions 10–13 with words from the text. Write **NO MORE THAN THREE WORDS**.

10 What would be uncovered if ice and snow levels decreased? ....

11 What would populate the newly formed environment? ....

12 How does human behaviour encourage foreign species to migrate to new environments?
....

13 What may reduce the speed of reproduction of local animals and plants? ....

UNIT AIMS

READING SKILLS
Identifying the writer's point of view
Scanning for synonyms
Identifying detailed information and
   scanning for facts

EXAM PRACTICE
Matching information
Yes/No/Not Given
Short answer questions

A

B

Identifying the vocabulary of opinions

1 Look at these images and answer the questions.
   a How do you think images A and B are connected with education?
   b The words in the list below have positive, negative and neutral connotations (emotional associations). Complete the table with words from the list that you would associate with each of the images A and B.

   healthy ▪ filthy ▪ happy ▪ starving ▪ well-fed ▪ abandoned ▪ neglected
   loved ▪ mistreated ▪ child ▪ miserable ▪ secure ▪ clean ▪ sick

Positive	Neutral	Negative

   c Write down as many synonyms for these words as you already know.
   d Look for more synonyms in a thesaurus.

Skills

Scanning for synonyms

2 Scan the passage on pages 79–80 about sport and physical activity and complete the table with synonyms for the key words in the heading.

facilitating	lifelong	participation	sport/physical activity

3 Rewrite the heading of the passage using some of the words in the table. Make sure the new heading is grammatically accurate.

Exam skills

Matching information questions

This type of question tests your ability to scan a text for detail by asking you to identify sections of the reading passage where you can find specific information. Before you scan the whole text, identify the key words in the questions and think of synonyms you might expect to find in the passage. You can then scan each paragraph for key words and synonyms to locate the information.

4 Which paragraph in the reading passage contains the following information? Write *A* or *B* next to each statement.

a a justification for giving school children the opportunity to practise a range of sports

b the main reason why people do not develop an early interest in practising sport

c research findings on the effectiveness of physical education in encouraging long-term interest in sport

d the reason why secondary school physical education programmes fail to encourage long-term involvement in sports

e the ultimate objectives of school sports programmes across the world

Facilitating lifelong participation in sport and physical activity

A According to the UK's Department of Education and Science (1992) the purpose of learning in physical education (PE) is to develop specific knowledge, skills and understanding, and to promote the physical development and competence that determines long-term engagement in sport and physical activity. Other countries make similar statements in policy documentation (see, for example, the contributors in Pühse and Gerber, 2005). In fact, in their survey of 52 countries around the world, Bailey and Dismore (2006) found that the promotion of lifelong physical activity was a universal aim of PE. Such expectations are not without justification, as a large body of literature suggests that PE – as the main societal structure for the promotion of regular physical activity during childhood – is the most suitable vehicle for promoting lifelong participation in sport and physical activity (Fairclough, Stratton and Baldwin, 2002; McKenzie, 2001; Shephard and Trudeau, 2002; Trudeau, Laurencelle and Shephard, 2004).

B In most developed countries children experience some form of regular curricular PE between the ages of 5 and 16 years (Hardman, 2001; Hardman and Marshall, 2009; Pühse and Gerber, 2005). However, many children do not maintain a lifelong involvement in sport or physical activity (Green, 2002; Roberts, 1996; Sallis and McKenzie, 1991). We suggest that this is, at least partly, ascribable to the poor quality of the PE experience. Ten years ago, Williams (2000) described primary PE in England as mixed in quality. After an investment of approximately £1 billion in PE and school sport, one government adviser was only able to say that 'a few schools are beginning to explore how they can realistically expect higher levels of achievement from a greater proportion of pupils, but this culture is proving slow to change' (Casbon, 2006, 15). This does not seem to be a local problem, as a number of international surveys have described similar situations elsewhere. Hardman and Marshall's (2009) worldwide survey, for example, revealed considerable cause for concern in terms of contributory factors for quality provision in both developing and developed countries. As a consequence, the foundation provided is so inconsistent that the start of the pathway is undermined. At the secondary level, PE is largely organized into short blocks of physical activities dominated by team sports that may not necessarily equip learners with the skills needed for lifelong participation in sport and physical activity (Fairclough, Stratton and Baldwin, 2002; Kirk, 2010; Penney and Jess, 2004; Trost, 2006). In fact, research in PE is increasingly concerned that the movement skills, knowledge and understanding essential for lifelong participation are not 'integral, explicit and valued elements of physical education' (Penney and Jess, 2004, 275). Roberts (1996) noted that PE teachers defend a 'sport for all' approach to curricular PE on the premise that by including a range of sports and activities more 'pupils would be able to find a sport at which they were competent and which they enjoyed and this would extend their participation into out-of-school and post-school lives' (1996, 50). Kirk's (2010) analysis suggests that a multi-sport approach continues to dominate and shows little sign of losing influence. However, Penney and Jess (2004) argue that it is important to broaden the skills, knowledge and understanding encompassed in PE curricula that claim to facilitate lifelong engagement in sport and physical activity.

Skills

Identifying the writer's point of view

Look again at the Skills section in Unit 4, page 34 on *Identifying opinions* to review the ways writers can indicate their point of view in a reading text.

Before you read the text in detail, you can use the following techniques to identify the writer's point of view:

1 Look at the heading of the text and any images that illustrate it. Do they have positive or negative connotations?
2 Scan the passage for adjectives and adverbs. Are they positive or negative?
3 Look for words that qualify the writer's statements for:
   a   truth – how probable does the writer think the evidence is? (e.g., *possible, probably, unlikely*)
   b   strength – how strong is the writer's claim? (e.g., *rather, somewhat, quite, decidedly*)
   c   attitude – what is the writer's feeling about the facts?
      (e.g., *unfortunately, optimistically, confidently*)

5 Read the following sentences a–f and write the letter A, B or C above the words that indicate whether the author is expressing:

  A probability
  B strength
  C attitude

Some sentences have examples of more than one of these.
  a   One surprising effect of a government-sponsored programme to promote better school meals was to increase the number of children bringing their lunch from home.
  b   Quite a lot of people believe that 'a healthy mind in a healthy body' is an essential guideline for a happy life.
  c   There is a significant difference between the concepts of 'education for health' and the 'impact of health on education'.
  d   It is a regrettable fact that many children throughout the world start the school day without breakfast.
  e   Research points to a strong likelihood that the recent increase in childhood obesity is a direct result of the abolishment of compulsory sports at school.
  f   Evidence indicates that education in healthy eating has only a slight influence on school children's choice of food.

6 Make the claim in sentences a–e *weaker* or *stronger* by adding a suitable adjective, adverb or modal verb from the list. Some words fit in more than one sentence.

> ~~may~~ ▪ extremely ▪ loose ▪ might ▪ distinctly ▪ striking

Example: Regular sports classes at school have a beneficial effect on children's health and academic performance.
Weaker: Regular sports classes at school may have a beneficial effect on children's health and academic performance.

a Research has found that there is a connection between literacy and nutrition.

Weaker: _____

b There is a difference in academic attainment between children who have stable families and those who are cared for by foster parents or in institutions.

Stronger: _____

c Children who learn to cook at school grow up to be more aware of the importance of a healthy diet.

Weaker: _____

d It is possible that children will learn to enjoy exercise if they practise sports at an early age.

Stronger: _____

e Children who are emotionally insecure are unlikely to perform well at school.

Stronger: _____

7 Which of the following phrases (a–l) from the reading passage report the findings of previous research and which express the views of the writers? Write *R* (research) or *W* (writers' claim) by each phrase.

a According to the UK's Department of Education and Science … _____
b Other countries make similar statements … _____
c … in their survey of 52 countries around the world, Bailey and Dismore (2006) found that … _____
d Such expectations are not without justification … _____
e We suggest that this is, at least partly, ascribable to … _____
f … Williams (2000) described … _____
g This does not seem to be a local problem … _____
h Hardman and Marshall's (2009) worldwide survey, for example, revealed … _____
i … research in PE is increasingly concerned that … _____
j Roberts (1996) noted that … _____
k Kirk's (2010) analysis suggests that … _____
l Penney and Jess (2004) argue … _____

Exam skills

Yes/No/Not Given questions

In this type of task you are asked to decide whether the statements in the question agree with the writer's claims or views. Remember that the answer NO means that the statement clearly contradicts the writer's claims. You must be careful not to confuse this with NOT GIVEN, which indicates that the writer has not expressed an opinion in the passage. In this case it is not possible to say whether or not the statement agrees with the writer's views.

8 Read the following passage on children's food choices. Do the following statements (a–e) match the claims of the writer? Write *YES, NO* or *NOT GIVEN*.

a   Children prefer to eat unhealthy foods. _____

b   Children are reluctant to eat more vegetables. _____

c   Scottish boys have a saltier diet than South-Asian children. _____

d   Adolescent girls eat fruit less often than boys of the same age. _____

e   School programmes to increase children's consumption of fruit and vegetables do not have a long-term effect. _____

Food choices are driven primarily by a child's familiarity with food and secondly by taste. Perceptions of which foods should be eaten in moderation and an understanding of balancing a diet appear to be weak. Where there is a wide variety of choice, children naturally choose the foods they like the most and even if more healthy foods are offered, a balanced meal may not always be chosen. Children and young people tend to leave the healthier elements of a meal while eating the less healthy items. Foods high in sugar and low in fibre, iron and vitamin A are frequently chosen and children's understandings of the dangers of a high-salt diet are also generally poor. Scottish children, and especially boys, have the highest likelihood of having a diet furthest from healthy-eating guidelines and minority groups, particularly South-Asian populations, have shown to be lacking in vitamin D and tend to eat more unhealthy foods and fewer vegetables than white Europeans.

Overall, children's knowledge of the positive benefits of fruit is greater than their knowledge of vegetables, and children tend to prefer fruit to vegetables. It is also easier to increase a child's consumption of fruit than it is vegetables. Apples and oranges are generally the most popular fruits although preference for both fruit and vegetables has been shown to vary with age and sex, with fruit intakes being higher among teenage girls than teenage boys and higher in England than in Scotland. Children participating in school fruit and vegetable schemes tend to have greater nutritional knowledge about fruit and vegetables than those not participating in schemes. Such schemes may be associated with a lower intake of fruit and vegetables in the home if parents rely on schools to provide children with their daily portions. Although schemes can increase fruit and vegetable intake in the short term, this increase tends not to be maintained once the intervention is withdrawn.

Reading Passage 10

You should spend 20 minutes on questions 1–13, which are based on Reading Passage 10.

Malnutrition and children's learning

A The impact of malnutrition on children's learning is not simply that they are tired and unable to concentrate in class because they have not eaten enough on a given day. Malnutrition in the first 1000 days – from the start of a woman's pregnancy until her child's second birthday – has a devastating impact on children's future potential. It restricts their cognitive development, means they are more likely to be sick and miss out on school, and reduces their ability to learn.

B This 1000-day window is a critical time for structural brain development. Good maternal nutrition is essential: pregnant or breastfeeding mothers who can't access the right nutrients are more likely to have children with compromised brain development and who suffer from poor cognitive performance. And once the child is born, nutrition continues to play a key role in ensuring the brain develops properly. But the effects of malnutrition on a child's cognitive development and education go beyond the biology of the brain. A child's nutritional status can impact on the experiences and stimulation that children receive. Parents sometimes treat a malnourished boy or girl differently because they are small, and this child is also more likely to miss school and key learning opportunities due to illness.

C The impact is not just on academic achievement. Malnutrition is associated with children having lower self-esteem, self-confidence and career aspirations. Malnourished children not only face direct damage to their bodies and minds, but are less confident to learn and aspire to change the situation they were born into.

D In the longer term, malnutrition can have a big impact on earnings when children reach adulthood. The effects of malnutrition on physical stature, the ability to do physical work, and on cognitive development, can lock children into poverty and entrench inequalities.

E Children who are malnourished go on to earn 20% less as adults than the children who are well nourished. But there is some evidence that the difference could be even larger – one study has estimated this earning deficit for malnourished children at 66%.

F This in turn means that malnutrition can act as a big barrier to economic growth. Estimates suggest that in low- and middle-income countries, the impact of malnutrition could decrease GDP by between 2% and 11%. This is partly a result of its impacts on educational development – as well as on physical productivity and health.

G This report presents new estimates of malnutrition's effect on GDP. By extrapolating a 20% reduction in earnings to a global level, this report shows that today's malnutrition could cost the global economy as much as $125 billion when today's children reach working age in 2030.

H Investments in the potential of future generations are more important than ever before. With mortality rates falling rapidly but fertility rates declining at a lower rate, developing countries will experience an increase in the size of their working-age population in the next few decades. Many countries will have two people of working age for every dependent. This presents them with a critical window of opportunity to boost economic development, known as the 'demographic dividend'.

I The IMF has predicted that seven of the 10 fastest growing economies in the next five years will be in Africa. Meanwhile, economists have identified the 'Next 11' countries – those that have the potential for stellar economic growth in the next decade. A common theme in each of these countries is the potential provided by their demographic structures.

J But to capitalize on the demographic dividend, developing countries must invest now in the health and skills of their future workforce. Investments made now in proven nutrition interventions could increase opportunities for millions of children to become more healthy and productive members of society. The next generation of children in developing countries could fuel improved innovation, prosperity and job creation.

K But if we fail to make that investment the consequences could be catastrophic. Not only would that leave a future public health disaster – with a huge burden placed on health systems by a generation of people left more susceptible to disease by malnutrition – but also an economic crisis. If countries are not able to take advantage of the opportunities presented by demographic changes, then in 50 to 60 years' time they will be left with a large cohort of elderly dependents without having generated the resources to care for them.

Questions 1–4

*Reading Passage 10 has 11 paragraphs, labelled **A–K**. Which paragraphs contain the following information?*

1 the psychological impact of malnutrition

2 the effect of parental attitudes on children's educational opportunities

3 the cost to the world economy of childhood malnutrition

4 the influence of childhood malnutrition on the national economy of individual nations

Questions 5–9

Do the following statements agree with the claims of the writer in the passage?

Write

   YES   if the statement agrees with the writer's claims.
   NO   if the statement contradicts the writer's claims.
   NOT GIVEN   if it is impossible to say what the writer thinks about this.

5   In developing nations, birth rates are falling at a slower rate than death rates.
   ....

6   All the countries with the most promising prospects for expansion in the next
   10 years are in Africa. ....

7   Malnutrition has a direct effect on both physical and intellectual development.
   ....

8   Poor nutrition during pregnancy does not affect the development of the child's brain.
   ....

9   It is essential for developing nations to devise strategies for taking care of the sick.
   ....

Questions 10–13

Answer questions 10–13 with words from the text. Write **NO MORE THAN THREE WORDS**.

10 How can the cognitive development of babies be assured before birth?
   ....

11 What is the main cause of absenteeism from school in underfed children ?
   ....

12 What factor most supports the future economic expansion of the 'Next 11'
   countries? ....

13 Who would benefit most immediately from effective nutritional programmes
   in developing countries? ....

Answer Key

Unit 1

1

Possible answers

a They're famous/celebrities/
   entertainers. He's/She's a singer/
   an actor.

b sports, exploration, politics,
   business, reality TV

c newspapers, magazines, radio,
   television, Internet, mobile texts,
   emails

2

exceptional, famous figure, superstar,
remarkable, Internet, controversial,
social media website, recognized
worldwide, video, reality TV

3

exceptional/remarkable, famous
figure/superstar, famous/recognized
worldwide

4

a ordinary
b unknown
c worker
d acceptable
e local

5

c

6

A celebrities, media, relationship,
   dependency, interests, challenge

B press, social media,
   photographers, radio, television,
   public profile, visibility

C sales, revenue, advertising,
   audience ratings, boosted

D conflict, media, privacy

E clash, digital science, online social
   media, rumours, press, reputation,
   photographic equipment,
   photojournalists, private,
   personalities, battles, newspapers,
   court cases

F court, judge, press, well-known
   figures, public interest, private
   lives, benefit, information

7

A vi
B vii
C ii
D viii
E iv
F iii

8

a press, social media,
   photographers, radio, television,
   advertising, audience,
   stories, gossip, information,
   communications, publish, images

b all nouns, except 'publish'

c press: media, journalists, reporters,
   newspapers
   social media: networking websites,
   online communities, Facebook,
   Twitter
   photographers: photojournalists,
   paparazzi
   radio: audio broadcasts
   television: TV, video broadcasts,
   small screen
   advertising: promotion, publicity
   audience: listeners, viewers,
   public, film-goers, spectators,
   theatre-goers
   stories: reports, articles, tales,
   accounts, news
   gossip: rumour, chatter, scandal,
   slander
   information: facts, data,
   knowledge, message, report
   communications: information
   technology, media
   publish: print, broadcast, circulate,
   distribute, publicize
   images: photos, pictures,
   illustrations

9

a needs, celebrities, media, not,
   conflict

b stars, advantage, publicity

c gossip, celebrities, successful

d famous people, no, right, privacy

e because, technology, famous
   people, more, difficulty, protecting,
   privacy

f large percentage, population,
   interested, private lives, public
   figures

10

needs/dependency/interests
celebrities/famous, influential, public
figures/people/stars, superstars/
high-profile, well-known personalities
media/press/radio/television/
newspapers
conflict/clash
advantage/benefit
publicity/advertising
gossip/rumours
successful/top-class
right/entitled to
privacy/private lives
technology/communications/digital
science/high-tech
difficulty/challenge
population/public

11

a False
b True
c Not Given
d False
e True
f Not Given

12

A
F
H

13

i e, g
ii e A, g F

14

a E
b C
c B
d D
f G

Reading Passage 1

Questions 1–5

1 B iii
2 C v
3 D vi
4 F iv
5 G i

Questions 6–10

6 F
7 F
8 T
9 T
10 NG

Questions 11–14
11 E
12 D
13 C
14 B

Unit 2

1
b tendency/trend

2
A percentages
B schedules
C areas
D tendencies
E eras
F ratios

3
juiperabtelegunerazeoirucremdeb
bats<u>Northumberland</u>oemormmport
mosl493wa<u>proportion</u>stermeluquest
asldinhaoloelbatskipszmxottrowetm
suejid<u>1900</u>kwqjsdnndndhoo

Possible answers
Northumberland – starts with a
capital letter, is in the first line. 1900
– is a number and a date.

4
1 twice
2 six (1970s, 1980s, 10 years,
21st century)
3 five
4 Paragraph C
5 It expresses an unfulfilled
condition. People in Australia and
the UK are not in the same room.

5
1900–1960 E
1970–1975 A
1976–1985 D
1986–1989 B
present C

6
place names: United States,
Australia, UK
periods of time: first decades of
twentieth century, 1970s, between
the late 1970s and mid-1980s, late
1980s, first 10 years of 21st century
technical terms: mainframe, desktop,
virtual environment, PC, mobile
phone, laptop, tablet

7
1 date – beginning of 1970s:
Paragraph A
2 technical term – mainframe:
Paragraph A
3 technical term – creating virtual
environments: Paragraph C

4 technical term – communication
software: Paragraph C

8
1 contest
2 aspect
3 provision
4 routine
5 rights

9
1 C
2 D
3 C
4 A

10
1 C and E
2 B and C
3 A and D
4 B and D

Questions 1–5
1 G
2 C
3 C
4 B
5 E

Questions 6–10
6 A
7 C
8 C
9 B
10 C

Questions 11–12
11 A and E
12 B and E

Unit 3

1

Possible answers
a clean: unpolluted, uncontaminated,
fresh, treated
b scarcity: shortage, lack of
c consumption: drinking, utilization,
use
d disease: sickness, illness, disorder,
contamination

Opposites
a dirty, polluted, contaminated,
stagnant, untreated
b abundance, excess, surplus
c conservation, non-drinking
d health, decontamination

2
Main topic: water
Sub-topics: consumption, clean

3
1 treated
2 50
3 50
4 30

4
1 surface water
2 untreated water
3 treated water
4 piped supply

5
a rope pump
b water, rope, wheel

6
1 wheel
2 PVC pipe
3 rope
4 washers

7
a on the rope
b at the top of the well
c below the water line
d at the top of the well
e below the water line
f up the pipe

8
1 information
2 included
3 excluded
4 concentration
5 public health
6 increase

Questions 1–6
1 unimproved sources
2 24
3 89
4 61
5 developing world
6 least developed

Questions 7–10
7 F
8 C
9 D
10 B

Questions 11–12
11 Democratic Republic of Congo/
Congo/DRC/Democratic Republic
Congo/DR Congo
12 Rwanda

Unit 4

1

Possible answers
a A international space station
B space shuttle

b A international space station was launched in 1998, is manned by astronauts from different countries, used for scientific experiments
  B space shuttle programme was launched by the US in 1981 and ran until 2011, used to transport astronauts into orbit and to the ISS
1 Restricted space – limited space in spacecraft, implications for size and weight of passengers
2 Expensive – space tourism only for the well-off
3 Exciting or dangerous – dangers of space travel
4 Health – physical limitations for passengers

2
A 3
B 4
C 2
D 1

3
1 c
2 b
3 a
4 d

4
a v
b ii
c iv
d i

5
See above

6
A iv
B v
C ii
D iii

7
A ii
B i
C iv
D v

8
1 C
2 B
3 D
4 B
5 A

9
i fact
ii opinion
iii fact
iv opinion
v fact

Questions 1–6
1 Paragraph C v
2 Paragraph D x
3 Paragraph E viii
4 Paragraph F vii
5 Paragraph G iv
6 Paragraph H i

Questions 7–10
7 YES
8 NO
9 NO
10 NOT GIVEN

Questions 11–13
11 B
12 C
13 D

Unit 5

1

Possible answers
a athletics/sprinting, volleyball, high jump
d health, competition, socializing, money
e commercial institutions (banks, alcohol, cigarette, sports equipment, health products manufacturers, airlines)
f advertising, publicity, commercial benefits, social responsibility, political reasons

2
i   track
ii   court
iii field
iv   track
v   court
vi   pool
vii mat
viii cross-country
ix   slope
x   pitch

3
sponsorship
athletic
cyclist
diver
promotion
financial
funding

4
a cyclist
b financial
c sponsorship, promotion
d divers
e athletic(s)

5
Paragraph A: first, afterwards, for, until, later, ever since
Paragraph B: before, following, first, second
Paragraph C: because, depends on, consequences, will result
Paragraph D: more famous, wider, colder, fewer, however, more exciting
Paragraph E: if, unless, whenever

6
a cities
b approval by their National Olympic® Committee
c Applicant phase
d city
e is adequately prepared and has the potential to organize the Olympic Games®

7
i   F
ii T
iii T
iv T
v   T

8
i   F
ii T
iii F
iv NG
v   NG

9
i   A
ii B
iii C
iv A
v   B

10
i   A
ii   C
iii B
iv   A
v   C
vi   B
vii C
viii C
ix   B
x   A

Questions 1–6
1 B
2 C
3 C
4 A
5 D
6 D

Questions 7–10
7 T
8 F
9 T
10 NG

Questions 11–14
11 B
12 A
13 A
14 C

Unit 6

1

Possible answers
a A nuclear family
  B extended family
  C tribe
b A the advantages and
    disadvantages of modern,
    nuclear marriages
  B the rise/fall of extended families,
    advantages/disadvantages,
    effect of economy and
    employment patterns
  C relationships within tribes,
    comparison with families, loss
    of traditional incomes/means of
    sustenance
c Modern familes
  Shrinking familes
  B Three generations in one home/
    The decline of the extended
    family/Grandparents at home
  C Tribes and families/Tribal living/
    The decline of the tribe
d/e 21st-century familes, working
    patterns, living conditions
  B cultures where extended families
    are the norm, comparison with
    other cultures, effect of economy
    on family size, advantages and
    disadvantages of extended
    families
  C tribal structures and relationships
    changing/traditional means of
    survival/changes in environment/
    economy affecting traditional
    livelihoods

2
Paragraph A: 1 S, 2 M, 3 S, 4 S
Paragraph B: 1 S, 2 S, 3 M, 4 S, 5 S
Paragraph C: 1 S, 2 M, 3 S, 4 S

3
A 2, 1, 4, 3
B 3, 2, 5, 4, 1
C 2, 4, 1, 3

4
See completed paragraphs

5
1 B, D
2 A, C
3 B, E

6
1 economic
2 psychological
3 communication
4 defensive
5 links

7
A ii
B iii
C iv
D vii
E v

Reading Passage 6

Questions 1–4
1 B and D
2 C and D
3 A and B
4 C and D

Questions 5–8
5 parenting
6 maternal
7 interaction
8 personal

Questions 9–13
9 G
10 A
11 F
12 B
13 E

Unit 7

1

Possible answers
a/b social networking/media
    websites/online/virtual/real-life
    friendships, Facebook, Twitter,
    Bebo, chat, computer-assisted
    communication, 'like', trend,
    tweet
c social networking n, media
  websites n, online adj/adv,
  virtual adj, real-life adj,
  friendships n, Facebook/Twitter/
  Bebo n, chat n/v, computer-
  assisted adj, communication n,
  like v, trend n/v (used on Twitter),
  tweet n/v

2
A creative, creativity, creation,
  recreate, recreation, recreational
B international, multinational
C intercommunicate, communicative,
  communication,

D interact, react, active, activity,
  action, interactive, interactivity,
  interaction, reactive, reactivity,
  reaction
E reorganize, disorganize,
  organization, organizational,
  reorganization, disorganization
F entertainment
G interrelate, relative, relation,
  relationship
H friendship
I multimedia
J antisocial

3
1 interact/communicate
2 relatives/relations
3 relationship/friendship
4 interaction
5 entertainment
6 multimedia

4
a unlikely
b disagree
c inaccessible
d misunderstand
e illogical
f abnormal
g unjustified
h deregulate

5
a disagree, dispute, forbid, prohibit,
  prevent
b deny, refuse, reject
c exclude, neglect
d deprive, remove, take
e contract, lessen
f avoid
g hide
h ignore, neglect

6
1 B
2 C
3 C
4 B
5 B

7
1 rarely see
2 old friends
3 products and services
4 social events
5 neighbourhood
6 sporting news
7 videos
8 business or professional
9 promote
10 dating

8
1 D
2 F
3 G
4 C
5 H
6 E
7 B
8 A

Reading Passage 7

Questions 1–5
1 F
2 NG
3 F
4 T
5 F

Questions 6–7
6 creativity
7 collaboration

Questions 8–13
8 B
9 E
10 F
11 C
12 G
13 A

Unit 8

1

Possible answers
a A quality of care in residential homes for elderly
  B what are the best residential options for the aged with disabilities or poor health?
  C should people be forced to retire at a certain age?
  D government policies and the cost of pensions
b No. Depends on attitudes to the older generation, availability of paid employment, mortality rates, economic environment, pension and health policies
c A negative (neglect)
  B positive (home)
  C negative (fights)
  D neutral (solution)

2

a positive: improved, health, longer, life expectancy, greater, potential, productive, contribution, society, better, nourishment, impressive, advances, increased, reasonable, extended
  negative: little

b can, doubt, might
c possibly
d emphasis at the beginning of a sentence:
  Improved health, longer life expectancy and greater potential for a productive contribution to society ...
  There can be little doubt ...
  Thus, it is reasonable to assume ...

3
Sentences 1 and 2 fact
Sentences 3 and 4 opinion

4
a exhausted
b obstructive
c weary
d ignorance
e deteriorate

5
a definite
b may
c slight possibility
d almost certainly
e no question

6
1 e
2 a
3 d
4 b
5 c

7
mentioned: a, b, c, f

8
l.3 aims – potential
l.5 is seen – potential
l.10 expectation – potential
l.22 suggests – doubt
l.23 can be – possibility
l.31 seemingly – doubt

9
l.1 care
l.2 promoted, purpose-built, community-based
l.4 support
l.5 independence, private
l.6 positive
l.8 self-contained, flexibly, available
l.10 security
l.11 control
l.15 satisfaction
l.17 valued
l.18 new, innovative
l.24 settling into
l.25 quality
l.26 good, very good, rose

10
a YES
b NG
c NO
d NG

11
1 B
2 A
3 C

12
1 a
2 c
3 c
4 g
5 d
6 e
7 b
8 a
9 f
10 e

13
1 population
2 generation
3 employment
4 financial
5 active
6 self-employed
7 part-time
8 pensions

Reading Passage 8

Questions 1–5
1 YES
2 YES
3 NO
4 NG
5 NG

Questions 6–9
6 B
7 C
8 D
9 A

Questions 10–14
10 pressure
11 stressful
12 physical
13 voluntary
14 social

Unit 9

1

Possible answers

a global warming, sea levels

b B, C, A – pollution produces global warming which melts the ice caps and raises the sea level and floods coastal cities

c Opinions vary: For – Global warming has accelerated since humans have started polluting the atmosphere with fossil fuels, industrialization on a large scale. Against – The climate has long-term cycles that are not necessarily affected by human activity.

2

a topic: sea levels/focus: changes, annual measurement of tides/ period of time: 100 years

b topic: sea-level rise/focus: rate of acceleration/period of time: since 2000

c topic: US east coast cities/focus: two-metre rise in ocean levels

d topic: sea levels/focus: rises/ period of time: 19th and 20th centuries

3

Dates/ Periods of time	Measurements	Geographical locations
1880 century/ centuries Ice Age 2100 today decades	8 inches one degree Fahrenheit tens of feet 20 feet 20 to 80 inches	Greenland Antarctica

4

a has risen

b is expanding

c will cause

5

a New York – 80 inches

b The Hague – 45 inches

c San Francisco – 42 inches

d Venice – 42 inches

6

a cause: as a result of, be susceptible to, caused, affected by

b effect: consequently, lead to

c more rapidly, on the other hand (NB *greater part* is not a comparison, but a synonym for *majority*)

7

a application, traditional knowledge, environmental changes

b application, implementation, utility, use

traditional knowledge, assets, technologies, skills, community environmental changes, climate change, modern conservation, environmental practices, conservation management tool, conserve, biodiversity, sustainable, ecological systems, structures, spiritual, cultural, heritage, values, traditions, indigenous ecological knowledge, customary, traditional roles, philosophy, local knowledge

c traditional island knowledge/ subsistence and traditional technologies/climate change/ modern conservation methods

d argued (l.6)

since then (l.8)

for instance (l.8)

as exemplified (l.9)

while (l.11)

to conserve (l.13)

to link (l.15)

not only ... but also (ll.15–16)

for instance (l.16)

which refers to (l.17)

because (l.21)

these examples (l.22)

8

a marine

b coral reef health

c Kiribati

d ecological

e guardian spirits

f village gardens

9

a coastal areas

b compatible

c traditional roles

d guiding principle

e ecological systems

Questions 1–4

1 Antarctic Peninsula

2 >2.5°C

3 glacier termini

4 14 000 km^2

Questions 5–9

5 2005

6 2007

7 Atmospheric circulation

8 2006

9 warming

Questions 10–13

10 rock and permafrost

11 flora and fauna

12 increases the opportunity/ opportunity for introduction

13 rapid climate change

Unit 10

1

Possible answers

a the effect of health and care on children's educational opportunities

b positive: healthy, happy, well-fed, loved, secure, clean

negative: filthy, starving, abandoned, neglected, mistreated, miserable, sick

neutral: child

c/d positive: healthy – fit, well, strong; happy – content, cheerful; well-fed – well-nourished; loved – respected, valued; secure – safe, protected; clean – (no appropriate synonym)

negative: filthy – dirty, grimy; starving – hungry, malnourished; abandoned/neglected/mistreated – deserted, ignored, unloved, uncared for; miserable – unhappy, sad, wretched; sick – ill, unwell, unhealthy, ailing

Note: child – no appropriate synonym

2

facilitating	lifelong	participation	sport/physical activity
promote promotion	long-term post-school	engagement involvement	physical education physical development PE team sports

3

The promotion of/Promoting long-term/post-school engagement/involvement in physical development/team sports

4

a B
b B
c B
d B
e A

5

a surprising C
b quite a lot B
c significant B
d regrettable C; many B
e strong B, likelihood A, direct B
f slight B

6

a loose connection
b striking difference
c might grow up
d distinctly possible
e extremely unlikely

7

a R
b W
c R
d W
e W
f R
g W
h R
i W
j R
k R
l R

8

a YES
b YES
c NG
d NO
e YES

Questions 1–4

1 C
2 B
3 G
4 F

Questions 5–9

5 YES
6 NO
7 YES
8 NO
9 NG

Questions 10–13

10 good maternal nutrition
11 illness
12 demographic structures
13 (millions of) children

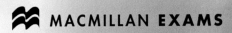

MACMILLAN **EXAMS**

DIRECT TO

Written by leading IELTS author Sam McCarter, Direct to IELTS provides a short and concise course that combines print and online materials for a more interactive learning experience

- Bands 6.0 – 7.0

- Eight topic-based units cover the skills required for the academic module of the IELTS exam plus grammar and vocabulary build-up

- A 'Writing Bank' provides detailed and focused practice including all task types found in the writing exam and annotated model answers

- The website includes four computer-based practice tests, written by an experienced exam writer, as well as downloadable worksheets to accompany the Student's Book

WITH FOUR **ONLINE** PRACTICE TESTS

IELTS

Student's Book

Sam McCarter

MACMILLAN
EDUCATION

www.directtoielts.com

The IELTS Skills Apps

Exam practice exercises and interactive tasks to help you develop the skills you will need to excel in IELTS.

- Written by Sam McCarter, the author of the bestselling *Ready for IELTS* and *Tips for IELTS*
- Each skill is explained and comes with examples and an interactive exercise
- Practise answering the full range of question types that you can expect to find in the IELTS exam

- A detailed overview of the IELTS exam
- Score yourself on the interactive 'Can Do' statement section
- A wide range of innovative and interactive exercises that help you work on the essential skills needed for the IELTS exam

Learn more at the Macmillan Education Apps
website: www.macmillaneducationapps.com